Bounce Back!

From Dreams To Reality
Faith Over Fear

Volume 2

Authored by:
DrStem Sithembile Mahlatini, EdD, LCSW

GLOBAL TRAINING COACHING & CONSULTING SERVICES, INC
ORLANDO

© 2024 by DrStem Sithembile Mahlatini

Co-Authors: Eva V. Mudambanuki; Mercy Chogugudza; Charlene Mahlatini and Chantelle Mahlatini; Patricia Bates; Shwanda Barnette; Dr James E. Bruce; Susan E. Casey; Zivai Ndhlovu; Vanessa Maldonado; Jessie Muzvidzwa ; Gary Moses ; Grace Quarshie ; Andy A. Charles **;** Tressa Perry ; Nicole Marange; Vanessa Farrell; J lucky Henry

All rights reserved. No part of this publication may be reproduced, distributed, or transmitted in any form or by any means, including photocopying, recording, or other electronic or mechanical methods, without the prior written permission of the author, except in the case of brief quotations embodied in reviews and certain other non-commercial uses permitted by copyright law. Excluded from this copyright are the contributing authors who maintain all rights to the material inside the chapter he or she wrote for this book.

Bounce Back : From Dreams To Reality- Faith Over Fear individual Vol 2 chapters. Copyright © 2024 by DrStem Sithembile Mahlatini,

Disclaimer—The advice, guidelines, and all suggested material in this book is given in the spirit of information with no claims to any particular guaranteed outcomes. This book does not replace professional consultation. Anyone deciding to add physical or mental exercises to their life should reach out to a licensed medical doctor or therapist before following any of the advice in this book. The authors, publisher, editor, and organizer do not assume and hereby disclaim any liability to any party for any loss, damage, or disruption caused by anything written in this book.

Library of Congress Cataloging-in-Publication Data
Names: Mahlatini, Sithembile, Author, et al.

Title: *Bounce Back : From Dreams To Reality- Faith Over Fear Vol 2*

LCCN: 2024916964

ISBN: 978-0-9905718-8-9

Cover Design: Faizan Siddiqui

Interior Design: Faizan Siddiqui

Editor: Erik Seversen

Global Training Coaching & Consulting Services, Inc

Orlando

Dedication

To those who dare to dream, who rise after every fall, and who embrace faith over fear. May this journey inspire you to transform your aspirations into reality? Your resilience ignites hope in the hearts of many.

To the dreamers who dare to envision a brighter future, who rise stronger after every setback, and who choose faith over fear in the face of adversity. This book is dedicated to you—those who believe in the power of resilience and the magic of persistence.

May your courage inspire others, and may your journey remind us all that every challenge is an opportunity for growth. Together, let us transform our dreams into reality, embracing each step with unwavering faith and determination. Your stories of triumph fuel the hope that lights the path for others.

Dreams do Come True.
Having faith is the only way to stop your fears from overpowering you.
Where there's faith, fear can no longer exist.

A Note to the Reader

Dear Reader,

Welcome to *"Bounce Back: From Dreams to Reality, Faith Over Fear."* As you embark on this journey with us, I want to take a moment to connect with you on a personal level. This book is not just a collection of stories, thoughts and ideas; it's a testament to the power of resilience, the importance of faith, and the incredible potential that lies within each of us. I am so honored and grateful to have had a chance to work with each of the contributing authors in this book.

Life is filled with ups and downs, and we all face challenges that can feel insurmountable at times. Whether it's personal struggles, professional setbacks, or unexpected obstacles, the journey can often seem daunting. However, it is in these moments of adversity that we discover our true strength. This book is designed to remind you that you are capable of bouncing back, no matter how hard life hits you.

Throughout the pages that follow, you will find stories of individuals who have faced their fears and transformed their dreams into reality. These narratives are not merely inspiring; they serve as blueprints for how we can navigate our own challenges. You will see that each person's journey is unique, yet there are common threads that bind us all—determination, hope, and an unwavering belief in a better tomorrow.

I encourage you to reflect on your own life as you read. What dreams have you set aside? What fears have held you back? This is your opportunity to reclaim those dreams and confront those fears head-on. Remember, it's never too late to start anew or to pursue the passions that ignite your spirit. The lessons within these pages are meant to empower you, to help you cultivate a mindset of resilience, and to inspire you to take actionable steps toward your goals.

As you dive into the chapters, allow yourself the space to be vulnerable. Acknowledge your fears, but don't let them control you. Embrace your dreams with open arms, and trust in your ability to turn them into reality. Each chapter is filled with insights, practical advice, and encouragement to help you on your journey.

Moreover, I want to remind you that you are not alone. Many have walked this path before you, and many will walk it after you. Lean into this community of dreamers and doers, share your experiences, and support one another. Together, we can create a ripple effect of positivity and resilience that extends far beyond ourselves.

In closing, I hope this book serves as a beacon of light during your moments of doubt and a source of inspiration as you chase your dreams. Embrace the journey, trust the process, and above all, have faith in yourself. You possess the power to turn your dreams into reality, and I am excited for you to discover just how much you can achieve.

If you too, are interested in co-authoring a chapter in our next Bounce Back Book please email drstem14@gmail.com or visit our website www.drstemmie.com

Contents

A Note to the Reader
By Dr. Stem Sithembile Mahlatini, EdD, LCSW 4

CHAPTER 1:
Unlocking Your Potential: The Journey from Dreams to Reality
By: Dr. Stem Sithembile Mahlatini, EdD, LCSW 9

CHAPTER 2
Dreams to Reality | Faith over Fear
By: J. Lucky Henry 29

CHAPTER 3
Activating Your Passions: From Paychecks to Purpose
By Shwanda T. Barnette, J.D. 48

CHAPTER 4
So Long, Insecurity
By Patricia Bates 62

CHAPTER 5
Life Is Like Climbing a Mountain
By James Bruce Sr., Ph.D. 72

CHAPTER 6
Rock Your Shine After You've Been Cracked Wide Open
By Susan E. Casey 80

CHAPTER 7
Intentionality and Clarity for Positive Action
By Andy Charles 90

CHAPTER 8
Rediscovering My Voice
By Mercy Chogugudza 98

CHAPTER 9
Values and Boundaries
By Vanessa I. Farrell 110

CHAPTER 10
Never Give Up—Growth Comes from Pushing
By the Tini Twins – Charlene & Chantelle Mahlatini........................121

CHAPTER 11
From Dreams to Reality
By DrStem Sithembile Mahlatini..126

CHAPTER 12
Me, Life, and God
By Vanessa Maldonado 139

CHAPTER 13
The Meaning of Faith Over Fear to Me
By Nicole Marange 148

CHAPTER 14
From Fear to Reality: Finances
By Gary Moses..158

CHAPTER 15
Unwavering Faith Amid The Storms
By Reverend Ever Vennah Mudambanuki..167

CHAPTER 16
Conquering Fear: The Rhythm of Faith Through Life's Seasons
By Jessie Muzvidzwa 177

CHAPTER 17
I Am a Miracle
By Zivai Mutsvene-Ndhlovu 189

CHAPTER 18
Simply Me
By Tressa Perry 201

CHAPTER 19
Faith Over Fear
By Grace Quarshie 208

CHAPTER 20
Faith Over Fear –The Journey to Freedom and Liberation
By DrStem Sithembile Mahlatini 219

Chapter 1

Unlocking Your Potential: The Journey from Dreams to Reality

By Dr. Stem Sithembile Mahlatini

To accomplish great things, we must not only act, but also dream; not only plan, but also believe.

—*Anatole France*

As I was thinking of what chapter or chapters I could write for this edition of our *Bounce Back* book series, I felt a chapter on unlocking your potential would be helpful in two ways: strengthening self-confidence and bringing clarity. In the work I do as a coach and counselor, I find that many who come to work with me are seeking the same two things—understanding themselves better and finding clarity on the next best steps in their life, career, and business. As you read this chapter, if something resonates with you or you find yourself in that place of desiring to elevate your life to the next level, let's work together. My contact information is at the end of this chapter.

May you enjoy this material and be enlightened and encouraged.

Understanding the Importance of Unlocking Your Potential

So, what is unlocking your full potential and why is it important? Unlocking your potential is the key to achieving extraordinary success in your life. It's about tapping into your unique talents, skills, and abilities to reach new heights. When you unlock your potential, you open doors to new opportunities and possibilities that you may have never thought possible.

To understand the power of unlocking your potential, you must first recognize that you are capable of far more than you currently believe. Often, we limit ourselves by doubting our abilities or succumbing to fear of failure. However, by shifting your mindset and embracing a growth mindset, you can break through these self-imposed limitations and unleash your full potential.

Unlocking your potential also involves self-discovery. It's about understanding who you truly are, what you're passionate about, and what drives you. By gaining clarity on your purpose and aligning your actions with your values, you can unlock a sense of fulfillment and satisfaction that will propel you towards success.

Have you ever felt like or thought that you could be so much more? Do you ever feel this need to unlock your potential? If yes, that's common for ambitious people, and it's also a sign that you can be so much more. I am happy you are reading this chapter. This is for you. At times you might even say, "I know that I have a lot of potential, but I am holding myself back."

Yes, you do have a lot of potential, and yes, you could be holding yourself back. You might not quite know what you want to do in life or how you can become the person you dream of being. So much human potential is wasted because people don't take the time and make the effort to figure out how they can reach their goals. However, you are different. You are reading this chapter to finally unlock your potential and start your journey from dreams to reality.

The good news is that you absolutely can unlock your full potential. It's going to take a lot of work though, and it does require quite a lot of time, but you can do it. I have worked with many men and women who were stuck and were ready to unlock their passion. The steps and questions I will share with you here are a part of what we explore in my coaching sessions. As you go through this chapter, make sure you have something to write with and something to write on so you can take notes and answer the questions.

You may have heard my TED Talk on YouTube titled, "YOHO—You Only Have One Life," in which I say, "Your future is important, and it deserves your full attention." Never forget that there's nothing you can't achieve if you set your mind to it. Let's begin the steps to unveiling your potential.

Step 1. What Exactly Do You Want to Do?

The most important question you need to answer is what exactly you want to do with your life. Who do you want to be? What do you want to achieve? To become the best version of yourself, you need to look at the big picture and know what matters the most to you. What are your personal values? What are the non-negotiables in your life?

When you have a somewhat clear idea of what you want your future to look like, you need to set clear and specific goals that will help you get there. Think about what you want your normal daily life to look like. What kind of career path would be good for you, and who are the people you want in your life?

Step 2. What Are Your Wildest Dreams?

To reach your highest potential, you must be honest with yourself and have the courage to say what you really want from life. What are your craziest, wildest dreams? Stop caring about what other people think of your ideas. If you want the American dream, or you want to be a successful business owner living in Bali, own that dream. Listen to your inner voice and take it seriously. You're not going to find the right path to your future if you hold yourself back and pretend to have smaller dreams than you really do.

Step 3. What Are Your Fears?

To unlock your potential, you need to know your fears. Everyone has them, and they tend to be the same: fear of failure, fear of the unknown, and feeling like you might miss out on something else important if you follow your dreams. But to really unleash your potential, you need to step out of your comfort zone. You need to be ready to face your fears. And do you know what? Many of these fears likely won't even happen. The world isn't as awful as you might think.

Usually, success stories follow the same pattern: someone decides to do something, they work hard and face challenges, and then one day, they make it big. The same applies to you. Don't be afraid of the bumps in the road—you'll get over them—and know, you have enough time to reach your goals.

Step 4. What Are You Good At?

I know you are good at many things, but you need to know your strengths so that you can see your potential. You have unique gifts, and you should be proud of them. List the things you are good at—be honest and not modest. You have already done a lot of things in your life, and you have many skills already. Working to become your dream self is always a journey of self-discovery. It takes time to understand who you really are and who you want to be, but once you know what you are good at, you also know what you can improve.

Step 5. What Skills Do You Need to Develop?

Once you have a clearer idea of what you want to do with your life and what your potential is, ask yourself what it is you still must learn. To become your best self, you will need to learn new skills. Perhaps you need to learn better time management or need to improve your emotional intelligence. Or maybe right now, you just need to focus on getting good grades. It all depends on who you are and what you want from your life. Learning new skills can be overwhelming at times but focus on making small steps forward, such as taking online courses, coming up with small challenges for yourself, or asking for advice from other people.

Step 6. Change Your Mindset and Beliefs

Your mindset matters. It can easily be the main reason someone settles for a less fulfilling life instead of going after what they really want. Because a good mindset is such a powerful tool, you should actively work on it. Build a growth mindset and keep an open mind for new challenges and new ways to learn. Make personal development a part of your daily life and know that you have true potential. You need to believe in yourself because you have the ability to make things happen and make those dreams of yours come true.

Step 7. What Is Your Timeframe?

Time flies when you are not looking, and that's why you need to be mindful of how you spend it. To set effective goals for yourself, you need to know what exactly you want to achieve and when. What can you do in the next month? By when should you have achieved the goal? What is a realistic timeframe for accomplishing your next goals?

Plan out each of your goals by writing down every step you think you need to take in order to meet these goals. It is important to be as clear as you can. What is the next step? How much time do you need for each task? How far do you think the finish line is from your current position?

Step 8. Stop Wasting Your Time

If you want to get things done and reach your fullest potential, you must stop wasting your time and learn to be efficient. Good time management is one of the most important things you can learn. It's way too easy to constantly be "on a break" or decide to do things "when you have more time." You have enough time already. I recommend you practice discipline and actively build good habits that help you to stick to your goals. Hard work is important if you have big dreams, but so is making time for them.

Step 9. Surround Yourself with Powerful People

Having the right people around you matters. I've repeatedly seen how people who have a lot of connections find opportunities much more easily than people who only hang out with the same old friends all the time. Getting to know new people is always a good thing, especially if they have experience in something you are interested in.

Start making new friends and new acquaintances and don't be afraid to reach out to someone who seems to be a little out of your league. If you want to unlock your potential, you need to reach higher. One effective step you can take is to find a mentor. A good mentor will help you with your goals and plans and share their valuable expertise with you. Searching for the right mentor might not be easy, but once you find them, you'll make progress fast!

Step 10. Learn from Inspiring People

It's good to know a lot of people in real life, but you can of course also learn from people you have never even met. If there are inspiring or successful people you admire, make sure to read their books, listen to their podcasts, or watch videos of them on YouTube. I'm not just talking about famous people here; perhaps someone interesting who you have been following on Instagram has a podcast you could start listening to.

I like to start my mornings by listening to motivational speeches on YouTube and music on my YouTube or Spotify playlists. Steve Jobs' commencement speech is one of my favorites on YouTube. If you want to start your days motivated, look for motivational speakers on YouTube or listen to interviews of the leading experts in your field. It only takes a little bit of time but can give you exactly the motivation you need.

Step 11. Constantly Push Yourself, Try Harder, and Try New Things

To reach your full potential and become the best version of yourself, you need to constantly push yourself. You need to try new things and set new challenges for yourself. The faster you can reach the next level, the better.

Often making the little changes in your life you know you should make isn't even that hard. You just need to do it. If something really is hard, simply focus on taking baby steps forward. The important thing is that you don't give up. If you just keep going, you have the potential to be in a much better place a year or two later.

Step 12. Look for Things That Are Holding You Back

To become better, you need to know what is holding you back. Sometimes it's a lack of certain skills, sometimes it's a lack of determination, and sometimes it's simply a lack of money. Whatever the problem is, you need to fix it.

Reaching your ultimate potential is about continuously learning and being honest with yourself. What is it that is holding you back? Should you go to sleep earlier, ask for a promotion, or set clearer short-term goals that help you reach your bigger goals? If you have a burning desire to make your dreams a reality, you need to allow for it to be easier for yourself to make constant progress. Having an effective set of daily habits that help you focus on your goals makes a difference.

Step 13. Remember That Time Is Everything

Again, time really matters. I have already talked about the importance of learning to be efficient, but most of the time, people spend time on things that really don't matter at all—like social media. To use your time better, the first step requires you to stop procrastinating. This is a massive problem; however, it's not the only course of action.

You also need to come up with ways to free up time for the things that really matter. If you, for example, want to work on your book for three hours a day, you need to find those three hours somewhere. Perhaps you could work fewer hours or meal prep on Sundays to free up time for writing? Maybe you could vacuum less often or combine your Pilates and TV watching? As you start looking for ways to save time on a daily basis, you'll notice that you actually have much more time than you thought.

Step 14. Don't Be Afraid to Do the Dirty Work

One common mistake that people make is to think that certain things are beneath them. Sometimes, though, to get better and to move forward, you need to be willing to do things that are uncool or "low-level." You need to be ready to do the work and pay your dues. Don't worry—this won't last forever, and it will pay off.

You also need to stop caring about the opinions of others or how fabulous their life looks compared to yours. When you give your best effort and have the courage to step out of your comfort zone, good things will happen. An internship that you don't want to do might easily lead to a positive outcome; perhaps you'll get a job offer right away, or in the future, a recruiter will be impressed by that addition to your resume. Remember—even a small amount of progress is still progress.

Step 15. Continuously Learn and Acquire New Skills

Nothing is more important to unlocking your potential than continuously learning and acquiring new skills. In today's rapidly developing and constantly evolving environment, it is essential to stay ahead of the curve and keep your skills and knowledge up to date. Whether it's learning a new language, taking a course, or mastering a new skill, the key to success is to never stop learning.

By continuously learning and acquiring new skills, you open up a world of possibilities for yourself. You become more valuable in the workplace, more confident in your abilities, and more equipped to handle new challenges and opportunities. It's a journey that requires discipline, dedication, and a willingness to step out of your comfort zone, but trust me—the rewards are well worth it. As you continue to learn and grow, you'll find that your potential is limitless, and that is truly the key to unlocking your full potential.

Step 16. Surround Yourself with Positive People

What do you feel when you're surrounded by people who lift you up and support you? A sense of positivity and motivation, right? Now, imagine the opposite. How do you feel when you're surrounded by negative, draining people? Drained, right? That's why it's so important to surround yourself with positive people. When you're surrounded by people who believe in you and support you, you'll be more motivated to chase your dreams and reach your goals.

Positive people can also serve as a source of inspiration and encouragement. They'll help you to see things from a different perspective and can help you to overcome obstacles that may be holding you back. On the other hand, negative people can hold you back and bring you down. They may discourage you from pursuing your goals and make you doubt yourself. They can also make it harder for you to stay motivated and focused.

So, make a conscious effort to surround yourself with positive people. Seek out people who inspire and encourage you, people who believe in you and your abilities. And, just as importantly, limit your time with people who bring you down. Remember—the people you surround yourself with have a direct impact on your mindset, attitude, and overall well-being.

Step 17. Take Calculated Risks

As I see it, taking calculated risks is a trait that is becoming more and more scarce in today's society. It's easy to play it safe and stick to what we know, but true success often comes from stepping out of our comfort zones and taking risks. It's important to remember that not all risks are created equally though. Jumping off a bridge with a bungee cord is a different kind of risk than investing your life savings in a new business venture. Calculated risks are calculated in the sense that they are weighed against potential rewards and losses, and the decision to move forward is made with as much information as possible.

It's also important to remember that taking risks is not a reckless act but a calculated one, based on a rational thought process and a well-informed decision. To truly unlock your potential, you must be willing to take calculated risks. Without taking risks, we limit ourselves and miss out on opportunities for growth and success. So, my advice to you is to assess the risks and rewards, gather as much information as possible, and act on the risks that have the potential to bring the greatest rewards.

Step 18. Believe in Yourself and Your Abilities

It is often said, "If you don't believe in yourself, who will?" This statement is so true because without self-belief you will be unable to accomplish anything meaningful. When you believe in yourself, you have confidence in your abilities, and you trust that you have the capability of achieving your goals. Self-belief is the foundation upon which all other aspects of personal development are built.

When you believe in yourself, you have the courage to take risks, the motivation to push through challenges, and the determination to achieve your goals. Believing in yourself also means having faith in your abilities, even when others doubt you. It means standing up for yourself and not being afraid to speak your mind. It means having the courage to be true to yourself, even when others disagree with you. So, believe in yourself, trust in your abilities, and go out and make your dreams a reality.

Step 19. Stay Open to Feedback and Criticism

No one is perfect, and we all have room for improvement. One essential way to unlock your potential and grow as an individual is to stay open to feedback and criticism. It can be difficult to hear negative feedback about ourselves, but it is crucial to be able to take constructive criticism and use it as a tool for growth. When you are open to feedback and criticism, you are able to gain a new perspective and learn from others, which can help you improve your skills and abilities.

It's important to remember that not all feedback will be positive, and it's essential to be able to separate constructive feedback from negative criticism. Constructive criticism is intended to help you improve, while negative criticism is meant to tear you down. By learning to distinguish between the two, you can use feedback to your advantage and make meaningful changes in your life.

Step 20. Learn from Failure

As famous businessman and former professional basketball player Michael Jordan once said, "I've missed more than 9,000 shots in my career. I've lost almost 300 games. Twenty-six times I've been trusted to take the game-winning shot and missed. I've failed over and over and over again in my life. And that is why I succeed." When you experience failure, it can be easy to get discouraged and give up, but it's important to remember that failure is a natural part of the learning process. Every failure is an opportunity to learn and grow. Each time you fail you gain valuable insights that can help you improve and succeed in the future.

As the saying goes, "Experience is the best teacher." When you learn from your failures, you gain a deeper understanding of yourself and the world around you. You learn what works and what doesn't, and you develop the skills and knowledge you need to achieve your goals. Don't be afraid of failure. Embrace it and learn from it. Failure is not fatal, but failure to change might be.

Step 21. Network and Build Relationships

Have you ever heard the phrase, "It's not what you know, it's who you know"? In today's fast-paced and competitive world, building relationships is more important than ever. Networking is the process of building and maintaining relationships with people who can help you in your personal and professional life. When you network, you create opportunities to meet new people, learn about new industries or job openings, and gain new insights or advice.

Building relationships takes time and effort, but it can pay off in the long run. It can help you find new job opportunities, advance in your career, and gain valuable insights and advice from others in your industry. Networking can take place in various forms, such as attending networking events, joining professional organizations, or even simply having coffee or lunch with a colleague.

The key is to be genuine and authentic in your interactions and always be looking for ways to help others. If you want to unlock your potential and achieve your goals, don't underestimate the power of building relationships. It can open doors for you that you never thought possible.

Step 22. Take Initiative (Calculated Risks)

Are you afraid of taking initiative? Do you find yourself constantly waiting for someone to tell you what to do or for the perfect opportunity to present itself? If so, it's time to push past those fears and take control of your own destiny. Taking initiative means being proactive, taking charge, and being responsible for the outcome of your actions. It means not waiting for someone else to give you permission to act, but instead, taking the lead and making things happen. It's about having the courage to step out of your comfort zone and make things happen, even when it may be difficult.

You see, taking initiative is not just about being productive. It's also about being accountable for your own growth and development. It's about taking ownership of your own life and being responsible for the direction that it takes. It's about being a leader, not just a follower. It's about making a difference and creating change. So, ask yourself: Are you ready to take initiative?

This is a lot, right ? Are you ready to take control of your own destiny? If the answer is yes, then it's time to take action. Start small, take baby steps, and soon you'll find that taking initiative comes naturally to you. Remember—the greatest rewards come to those who take the greatest risks, so don't be afraid to step out of your comfort zone and take the initiative to create the life you want.

Step 23. Embrace Adaptability and Change

You see, in the end, the ability to embrace adaptability and change is one of the most crucial skills for unlocking your potential. The world is constantly changing and evolving, and the ability to adapt to these changes is essential for success. COVID-19 was a game changer. This experience allowed all of us to embrace adaptability.

Embracing adaptability means being open to new ideas, new ways of doing things, and new perspectives. It means being willing to let go of old ways of thinking and doing things that no longer serve you. It also means being resilient, flexible, and able to pivot and change direction as needed. In today's fast-paced and ever-changing world, the ability to adapt is more important than ever. Those who embrace change and adapt to new situations will be the ones who are best equipped to succeed in the long run.

Step 24. Stay Motivated and Persistent

There will always be people who try to discourage you, bring you down, or tell you that you can't do it. Stay motivated and persistent. Don't let anyone or anything stand in the way of your goals.

Understand that setbacks and obstacles are a natural part of the journey towards success, but it's important to not let them defeat you. Stay motivated by focusing on the end goal and remember the reasons why you started in the first place. Persistence is key, as it allows you to push through challenges and keep moving forward, even when things get tough. Believe in yourself and your abilities and don't give up on your dreams. With a motivated and persistent attitude, you can accomplish anything you set your mind to.

Step 25. Stay True to Yourself

Examine your own values. Your values will guide your personal interests and behaviors, so it's worth taking some time to figure out what they are. Know that your values and your beliefs may change over time, and this is okay. Your list of values and beliefs won't remain static, and that's fine. The point is to check in with yourself and clarify your values. Stay true to yourself; do not hide your character or preferences. Be you, be free, and work towards always being the best version of yourself.

Final Thoughts on Unlocking Your Potential

Unlocking your potential is not easy, but it can be the best thing you do for yourself. You have so much untapped potential. Don't let small fears hold you back. I am very excited for you. Following the steps I mentioned above will hopefully make your journey clearer and easier. It is time to shift from dreams to reality with faith over fear.

It is time to start changing your life today. Set the right habits for yourself that you know will help you. Set clear goals that you can work on. Make sure that your daily routine benefits both your goals and your own well-being. I also want you to know that if you need it, I am here to provide you with support coaching and cheer you on. You can find more information on my website.

You never know—your life could be completely different a year from now, let alone ten years from now. Great things can happen at the most unexpected times if you just dare to try and see what you are capable of. Unlocking your potential is not a one-time event; it's a journey that requires consistent effort and dedication.

Before I finish this chapter, let me take the opportunity to invite you to be a co-author and publish with us in the *Bounce Back* book series. I now publish a *Bounce Back* book yearly and hold a book launch at our Bounce Back Empowerment Conference. If you have ever thought of writing a book, or you are a published author looking to expand your reach, I would like to invite you to join the *Bounce Back* author family. Email me at drstem14@gmail.com for more information or connect with me at www.drstemmie.com.

Be encouraged!
Dr. Stem Sithembile Mahlatini

Originally from Zimbabwe, **Dr. Stem Sithembile Mahlatini** is a confidence coach, resident, and owner of Global Counseling and Coaching Services, Inc. and founder of The Empowerment Academy, an online platform with life success programs, workshops, seminars, and books. Her mission is to inspire, empower, and educate others to live stress-free, successful lives through her speaking engagements, books, seminars, workshops, counseling, and coaching services. In addition, she hosts The Dr. Stem Show Radio, Television, and Podcast, which is an educational, empowerment, and encouragement show. You can find her shows on YouTube and all podcast platforms.

Drawing on her background as a licensed psychotherapist, Dr. Stem offers people practical advice on how to tap into their limitless power to change their lives, overcome roadblocks, and aspire to be better than the circumstances that surround them. For businesses, she provides cutting-edge training and coaching programs to help business leaders and employees break through personal and environmental barriers to maximize their success in all areas of their lives. Her lifelong goal is to continue to help others build unshakable confidence to be winners at home, work, and business. Her motto is: "Each day is an opportunity to become more confident, successful, and happy."

Websites: www.drstemmie.com

www.drstemspeaks.com

www.womenyouthservices.com

Chapter 2

Dreams to Reality – Faith over Fear

By J. Lucky Henry

The presence of fear does not mean you have no faith. Fear visits everyone. But make your fear a visitor and not a resident.

Max Lucado

I am going to tell you how I became a millionaire...

After what felt like the longest 30-minute drive of my life, we arrived at an office north of Boston and walked in to be greeted by mid-level staff dressed in business casual mixed with work from home attire as the pandemic had obviously caused an identity crisis for the workplace wardrobe. My business partner and I shook hands and engaged in small talk that I generally abhor but today more than ever I was about as interested in it as a cat is in taking a bath. However, I remained cool, smiled and tried my best to hide my impatience. "Just hand it over" I thought as the sun began to pour in behind us. I felt this was a divine moment and for a second I expected an announcement that I had reached a new checkpoint in this game called life, but was I making this a bigger deal than it was? I'm sure it wasn't his first time... but it was definitely mine. When he finally extended his arm to hand over what we came for my martial artist reflexes betrayed me and reached for the envelope way faster than I wanted too. Naturally, this prompted him to make some joke I don't remember, I laughed along (or maybe even at myself) before immediately opening the envelope to see if this moment would feel exactly like I dreamt it would. Once I pulled out the contents, I knew that my dreams paled in comparison as I saw a check with my company's name printed on it, for an amount that exceeded $700,000 I had to fight the urge to smile from ear to ear. This moment was an accumulation of the pan I set in motion two years ago. This moment was bigger than just this check; it was confirmation of what I believed about myself and this world. Which is that when you place your faith over fear, you can turn your dreams into reality.

When we added that $700,000 with the sale of one of our properties for $200,000 and all the rent and other income, the total amount my company received that year exceeded $1,000,000. This iconic moment wasn't the moment I became a millionaire but it was the first year $1,000,000 went through my business. As I write these words I am not yet a millionaire... However, if you are reading them then I am.

Let me explain, I had a dream of collecting $1,000,000 in a 12 month period and cashing a $500,000 check three years later and I accomplished both of those. I believe I would have done it sooner if I was more specific about what I wanted and how I wanted to get it. I set my eyes on becoming a millionaire by 35 shortly thereafter.

In this chapter I'll tell you a little bit about me, I'll share my seven step plan with you as to how I became a millionaire before you read this and I'll even let you know what my next major goal is! I have never actually shared this with anyone outside of my trusted circle, but Dr. Stem is in my trusted circle and she is so persuasive that there was no way I could say no...

Every Good Boy Does Fine... Any musician instantly recognizes that mnemonic as it's one of the first phrases you learn when beginning to read music. The first letter of each word is the note for each line in the treble clef. Thanks to my parents insisting on violin lessons from 5-6 years old and piano lessons from 9-10 years old I was familiar with it and could read music at a beginner level at least. Fast forward to my Junior year in college I'm hanging out with one of my best friends Kevin Clark who was attending Berklee college of music at the time and I was inspired by a late night jam session he was having with a few friends and decided I wanted to learn the saxophone and join the jazz band at my school.

The next day I was signing a loan to finance a saxophone from some store I found online in the middle of nowhere. I took it home and dove straight into creating atrocious noises that were accompanied by spit flying everywhere. When I found out when the jazz band rehearsed, I showed up wearing navy sweats with my sax in hand, was promptly welcomed and expeditiously dismissed. Unbeknownst to me they didn't teach you how to play the instrument they taught you how to play Jazz songs for performances. I was the equivalent of a high school freshman trying out for a starting spot on a college roster. My inner competitor kicked in and I attempted to strike a deal with the instructor. I proposed that if I could learn to play the instrument in time I could join and be a part of their next performance. Miraculously he agreed, and I had less than a semester to learn the instrument then learn the songs and then perform…

There was no doubt in my mind I would accomplish this goal. Despite being an amazing call of duty player at the time I traded in all the gaming hours for 1 on 1 "sexy" time. I was consuming hours of YouTube already on a daily basis but now I changed from silly pranks and sports highlights to saxophone how to videos, classic blues, and smooth jazz. Saxophone became my number 1 priority for the remainder of that semester. Therefore, I couldn't spend hours hanging out with my student athlete friend anymore. I needed to be working on my new craft and hanging out with other musicians.

One of the most fortunate occurrences was being friends with Molly because without her I would have never been overwhelmed with this feat. She gave me feedback, helpful tips and even let me get copies of the music the band was playing so I could "catch up" and boy did I have a lot of catching up to do.

After about 3 weeks I could play most of the parts for two of the songs the band was rehearsing. I showed up to rehearsals anticipating needing to put on a solo performance as some sort of audition and was already beginning to sweat as I walked in and everyone was warming up on their instruments, playing scales and doing breathing exercises. I remember the teacher asking me if I felt ready and I said yes, while thinking to myself: "I am most definitely not". Molly even vouched for me and said I had progressed a lot and was able to play so much better than just 21 days prior. Her affirmation of my results gave me comfort but what gave me more comfort was that I didn't have to do a solo performance in front of the group, instead I was allowed to join practice and play along. If I made any mistakes, they would obviously be apparent so whenever we got to a piece I didn't know I pretended to play and only played what I knew. This was a bit sneaky but looking back I'm sure the teacher not only knew but appreciated my efforts to play within my range. After rehearsal I was officially initiated into the band.

During the weeks leading up to the performance solos were handed out to the standout performers and naturally my inner competitor kicked in and I wanted one. After handing out several I realized I wasn't going to get one because the remaining ones were the hardest and those were going to two "ringers" that were brought in to fortify our sound on performance day.

My dream is now moments away from becoming a reality, bright lights blind us as we sit in our all-black attire, instruments in hand before an anticipatory crowd. I have been under the lights before, but this is different. There are no signs with my name on it, no pep rally bands, and no cheerleaders. Just silence, our maestro waving their arms and we begin.

I play my absolute best, I am focused, in the zone and simply put just grooving. The fortifier ringers were absolutely incredible, and the solos were inspiring. Then it just happened, I didn't plan it, I never even rehearsed it. It was like the accumulation of all the practice hours, the inspiration from the night I spent at Berklee watching that initial jam session, my inner competitor and the right moment. The song ended and there were twelve counts of unscripted melodic notes coming from my saxophone that nobody was prepared for, not even me. The crowd burst into applause (as they did after every song) but this one was special to me, even though they had no idea what I had just done. I nervously looked to my right to find Molly's excited gaze staring at me and telling me "whoa that was nice". Followed by a fist bump from one of the fortifiers.

As we prepare to dive into the 7 step plan we have to acknowledge the 3 truths that must be understood and accepted.

1. **You already have half the skills you need**

    Our brains, our heart and souls know more about what we are capable of than we do. They can draw on our past experiences and produce insight, competence and results in areas we didn't think possible. Sometimes we are privy to the obvious connections like knowing how to read music for the violin, learning finger dexterity with the piano and lung capacity from swimming were all skills that transferred over to the saxophone quite well.

2. **Time will pass whether you accomplish your dream or not.**

    The recital was going to happen and the semester would eventually come to an end regardless of whether I joined the band or not. However, some dreams might not happen without you because they are your creations for the world. For example, this chapter and my upcoming book wouldn't exist if I don't create them. However, tomorrow is going to happen whether I accomplish my dreams or not. We all have the ability to accomplish our dreams and in this life your decision on this journey will determine whether you carry all your potential with you to the grave or you convert that potential into tangible results in your lifetime.

3. **You need to be self aware and self defining**

I am a Sagittarius born in the year of the snake with an extremely high DI and substantially low SC DISC personality yet all of that means nothing compared to who I believe I am. When I first started my real estate career at Keller Williams, I got the idea that I wanted to use video marketing as a way to grow my brand and generate leads. This idea was met with resistance from the offset. I was told by colleagues and office managers "slow down" or "You don't need to make a video everyday" I won't even repeat what they heckled at me when I vocalized my aspirations of selling luxury real estate.

Fast forward and it's been almost a decade since I began my real estate career. I now have the largest realest channels on YouTube, and I am the founder of the first black owned luxury real estate brokerage in Boston.

Now lets dive into the 7 step plan

1. **Internalize The Dream**

You need to have a clear understanding of what you are accomplishing. Why it is a necessity and how you will feel when you realize it.

When I say I want to be a millionaire what does that mean? We know I already had a million dollars flow through my company in 1 year but that didn't make me a millionaire. Do I need to have it in the bank in order for it to count? Forbes calls people Billionaires based on their net worth not solely on their liquid assets. Thus I decided I wanted my net worth to exceed 1 million dollars by 2024.

Simply put, net worth is assets - liabilities.

A basic example is if you have $1,000,000 in the bank, a $200,000 personal loan balance and $50,000 in credit card debt then you would have a million liquid with a net worth of $750,000 after accounting for liabilities.

Have you ever had a dream that was so vivid it became almost tangible or palpable? I have found that to be the level of intensity required to accomplish the big dreams in life.

2. Set Momentable Goals

Our world and by all accounts the universe works in such a way that a moving object will continue to move in the same direction until met with equal or greater force.

Getting in a rhythm is beneficial to me emotionally, mentally, physically and financially. Nothing gets me more fired up than vigorously attacking a checklist that will lead me to my goals. However, before I can assault such a list I must create it. Then put it in the order that makes the most sense. Imagine having all the ingredients for a cake and each instruction is on a single flash card. Then along comes life in the form of a random gust of wind through your kitchen window and blows all the unnumbered cards everywhere. If you plan to successfully bake that cake you are going to have to figure out the correct order of steps. One way to do that would be to work backwards, start with the step that says the cake is finished and think about what the best next step would be just before that and then the one before that.

As I thought backwards about my millionaire goal, I realized I needed to answer the question: What did "millionaire me" make for income? Is it passive or active or leveraged? This led me to understand I would need to increase my cashflow, have assets that gave me equity, and have scalable businesses that could be sold.

Active - requires me to be involved almost daily in order to function
Leveraged - a system that only requires me to manage it

Passive - a system that requires almost nothing from me to function

Conservatively assuming I could only sell each company for 1x EBITDA (Earnings Before Interest Taxes Depreciation and Amortization) I decided I would expand my real estate sales business to generate an active $250,000/yr by opening a brokerage. Grow my media company to about $125,000/yr leveraged by focusing solely on YouTube content. Increase the equity in my real estate holdings to about $500,000 through a new purchase and strategic renovations on my current property. Also I would start and build a passive hospitality company that generates $125,000

Enter short term rentals and specifically of the single room occupancy variety. Airbnb, VRBO, Furnished Findings and a whole other suite of platforms. The plan was simple: start with what I can control.

Before I can get to $125,000/year I need to set smaller attainable and motivating goals that allow me to gain momentum

Month 1 - Paint rooms, buy furniture, take pictures of rooms and sign up for air bnb.

Month 2 - Test out the platform to see what I can earn. I made $1500 off of a bedroom I had previously rented for $1000/month

Month 3 - I earned $1800 off that room and $900 off of another bedroom that I previously wasn't collecting rent from.

Month 3 - Create systems for management and make enough to cover the mortgage. I was able to cover it using 3 of the 6 bedrooms.

Month 5 - Rent 5 bedrooms at once and test the management systems. All 5 bedrooms got booked and management systems did well under stress.

Month 6 - Earn over $10,000 from air bnb and earn super host status... I think you are seeing the point here. I crushed that goal too!

It took 6 months to achieve the correct monthly income to hit my yearly goal. Now I need to sustain this average for a year. It would have been impossible to go from $0 to $10,000 in a month mostly because I had no idea what I was doing. It required learning and help from others which I'll explain soon. However, now that I am experienced in the matter when I buy my next property, I can take it to $10,000 in 2 months or less.

My approach to real estate sales and the event company were equally as methodical. I decided every dollar from real estate would be used to pay off bad debt and go into savings. Then I would live off of whatever I made from the event and media company. While the Airbnb profit was reinvested into the property or set aside to buy another property. This approach allowed me to increase the equity in my home as I updated bathrooms, redid the basement, landscaped etc; while simultaneously saving and increasing my cashflow. I was emboldened by every milestone and like a snowball coming down a hill my certainty and clarity grew into an unstoppable energy headed towards it's target.

3.   Determine The Cost

Once I knew what I wanted and what was required to pursue it I needed to discover what the true cost of my dreams would be. I remember when I used to fight kickboxing I would often give up "saxy time" (I didn't even own a saxophone yet), drinking alcohol and late nights for weeks before the fight. This was part of the cost, I also needed to train twice a day which meant I gave up free time, friends, and fun. My meals consisted of low sodium and carbs 2 weeks prior to every fight so that I would lose water weight and be as lean as possible for the weigh-ins. Once those were over, I would have carbs the day before the fight to regain my weight and strength.

As I reflected on my path towards my dreams, I realized it would cost a fortune...The list of sacrifices became burdensome and included:

    A.   TV time

    B.   Alcohol

    C.   Ignorance

    D.   Diffidence

    E.   Self-neglect

    F.   Fear of success

    G.   My significant other

    H.   Social media scrolling

    I.   Weekends with friends

    J.   Avoiding tough conversations

    K.   Opportunities that don't fit my plan

Many of these are permanently gone from my life and some are temporary modifications for this specific point in time. Everyone has their own vices and demons to conquer; these were mine. Individually these things may not be bad and sometimes they might even be necessary. However, my self-assessment led me to understand this is the cost of achieving my dreams and I knew I was ready to pay it!

4. Time Block

Step 4 is the apex of this plan, it will feel like the point when a roller coaster is approaching it's highest point, it begins to slow down and you begin to question if it's broken, or if this is even a good idea.

I felt overwhelmed by this part of the plan because it requires creativity and commitment in droves and if you mess it up the whole plan can begin to feel pointless and your dreams unattainable. Nonetheless, I was able to describe a way to fit my to-do list in my calendar with sufficient time to still eat and sleep. Remember that imaginary cake we were baking? Well, I actually attempted to make a red velvet cake as a thank you for an amis-amant of mine who loves desserts. The cake was not the best in the world, but the cake was indeed a cake. I had never baked anything in my life but when I looked up how to make a red velvet cake there were tons of recipes and by simply following them anyone can make a cake that actually tastes good.

This I believe is the same for finite goals, and which is why this step is the crescendo of the plan. I basically created a recipe for my goals. I had the steps but they needed to be executed in a specific order and at certain times of the day. I couldn't make phone calls to potential clients at 10pm but I could shoot videos then. It would make no sense to workout at the gym in the middle of the day, since it's open 24 hours and I could use that daytime to show properties. Sending emails became an early morning late in the evening task while phone calls became the during the day task.

By time blocking parts of my calendar for specific types of tasks and then filling them in with mini checklists that I generated from working backwards on my goals I created a recipe that I could follow that would lead me straight to the realization of my dreams.

5. Preemptively Boost Productivity

There are three ways I have found to jumpstart, maintain and improve my productivity. Public accountability, finding a worthy opponent and choosing an appropriate arena.

As we delve into this I want to make one thing clear, my goal isn't to be busy it's to be productive and extract results efficiently. There is a saying that goes: "if you want something done you should ask it of a busy person". I see the merit in that statement, and I also see the merit in asking a lazy, but smart person. Which is the category I believe I fall into. Much like a puppy in a cage, I'm bored and need stimulation preferably in the form of competition. Otherwise, I would lay around and do nothing all day. This is why I strive in environments that don't punish controlled chaos and simultaneously reward results.

Public Accountability

We all have a way we want to be seen by others and in some of us that image is uber important. Personally, I am a fan of congruency, and I will make sure the world sees a version of me that is as awesome as I see myself. When Muhammed Ali told the world, he was the greatest he had no choice but to live up to it. On a much smaller scale I do this with goals and milestones. I have posted several goals publicly on social media and the embarrassment of not being true to myself is enough to jumpstart any plan of mine.

Worthy Competition

Another big motivator for me is not letting people I care about down. My other best friend Jesse M Fowler VI is equally as obsessed with self-improvement as I am. This drives a lot of competition between us that pushes us to new heights. We both believe in the other so much that if one of us declares a goal we know the other will sacrifice time and allocate resources towards helping each other. Engaging with someone that can beat me on their best day or my worst day ensures I have to show up at my best if I even want this to be competitive. From football to Fortnite and cafeteria jokes to credit scores we push each other to be better because we respect each other's abilities and therefore bring our best efforts creating an iron sharpening iron type of environment.

The Environment

Lastly, I needed to make sure I'll choose as many battlegrounds as are conducive to my style. Air bnb guests have no idea how crazy unorganized or organized things are behind the scenes. They just know when they show up at their appointed time all that matters is the experience they have during their stay. A hard deadline that I must meet daily and a clear rubric that must be met to achieve Superhost with no penalties for being chaotic is an environment in which u can thrive. Superhosts don't earn their status for simply being nice, or just because they have been hosting for a long time. The title is bestowed upon those who meet the results criteria. This is how I became a super host in less than 90 days.

6.   Sprint Don't Think

"There is a time for thinking and a time for doing and you best not get them confused" is what I would tell myself when it's time to work "in" the business rather than "on" the business. My late mentor Mr. Edwards taught me many lessons about business and the world and some of the greatest lessons came from the books he had me read. Once such book was the e-myth revisited and it talked about this concept. Simply put, "on the business" means thinking and "in the business" means doing.

At this point in the plan, it's do time! Shutoff the thinking brain and sprint through the checklist items on your recipe as fast as you can. Focus on the task at hand and don't get bogged down second guessing or trying to improve the strategy during this time. Momentarily, you are no longer the general you are a soldier with marching orders. You have been pointed in the right direction now shoot what's in front of you. If you find yourself overthinking remember to: keep it simple, stupid (I trust you understand this is an acronym and I'm not calling you names).

7. Evaluate, Tweak and Repeat

My football coach taught me one of the most important business skills I needed.

Imagine this you are competing against another team and everyone on your team is counting on you to make the right move just like you have practiced dozens of times before. Then when the moment comes you make a mistake in front of your teammates, family, friends and your entire school. Embarrassing right? Now picture having the entire weekend trying to live down the moment and then coming back to school on Monday only to have Coach P. put that exact sequence up on the projector in front of your teammates and play it a few times in slow motion before rhetorically asking you "What are you doing here?"

That's all it took in those days to make me H.A.M. (Humble, Accountable, Motivated) for the next time. I hated those moments, but they taught me how to make tweaks and how to be a winner.

Nobody can be harder on me than I am on myself because I have been taught and embody the principle that I must take accountability not just for the mistakes but for the corrective actions.

The acceptance of these truths and the implementation of this 7-step plan is what made me a millionaire before my 35th birthday and the foundations as to why I will be worth over 10 million before I am 40.

Steve Jobs famously said *"you can't connect the dots looking forward only looking back"* Well If you knew this information 5 years ago how different would your life be right now? I used to ponder that question all the time until I realized that knowing without doing was pointless. So I began asking myself how different would life be if I had acted on this information 5 years ago. However, I may enjoy the fantasy of the what if, it is just that a fantasy. The better exercise would be to write down the one thing that would have the biggest impact for you right now. Then do it!

J. Lucky Henry

Meet J. Lucky Henry, Real Estate Agent who is a dynamic entrepreneur who, by the age of 35, has charted a journey marked by the creation, triumph, and even setbacks of over a dozen companies. His resilience, innovation, and leadership have been the cornerstone of his success, attributes nurtured by his upbringing in Aruba and his professional athletic pursuits.

For nearly a decade, J. Lucky has immersed himself in the realm of real estate, wearing the hats of both investor and broker. With a portfolio spanning North America and the Caribbean, his family's properties underscore his deep-rooted connection to the industry.

Based in Boston, where he resides, his team serves a global clientele, facilitating seamless transactions and investments in Greater Boston by providing unparalleled market insight and guidance.

Currently proficient in seven languages with a goal of mastering ten, J. Lucky embodies a commitment to fostering cross-cultural understanding and communication—an invaluable asset in today's interconnected world.

Beyond business, J. Lucky is a passionate advocate for community empowerment and catalyzing change. He champions the belief that communities should have ownership and influence in areas such as Trades, Real estate, Art, and Politics (TRAP), actively working towards this vision through initiatives like TRAP Haus Boston and his involvement in local civic groups, including serving as the secretary of the District 7 Community Fund.

When not setting real estate sales records or engaging in civic endeavors, J. Lucky channels his energy into his upcoming book, "Real Estate Dreams & Nightmares: My Million Dollar Journey," a captivating exploration of his experiences and insights, available for preorder now and set to launch on November 26th, 2024.

Chapter 3

Activating Your Passions: From Paychecks to Purpose

By Shwanda T. Barnette, J.D.

Never Give up on what you really want to do. The person with big dreams is more powerful than one with all the facts.

– Albert Einstein

"So, what do you do for a living?" These words can carry so much weight and often are attached to some degree of pride or shame. Whether you are a stay-at-home caretaker or an award-winning artist, there is a feeling that stirs inside each one of us when asked to disclose that part of our "being." So much of how we define our identities in society is tied to our careers or the lack thereof, and I am not immune to that pressure. After years of the power struggle between what I was expected to do professionally, and who I actually am, at the age of 40, I made the decision to bring those two things into alignment. I believe self-actualization is a lifelong journey, and even the tiniest steps we take to silence the external noise and the internal self-doubt, to follow what's truly in our hearts, take us one step further on that journey. I begin by acknowledging this is easier said than done and yet I believe this process is necessary for moving beyond the rigmarole of "just trying to survive" this life and actually thriving in it. I am sharing my journey, which is still very much a work in progress, with the hope that it will inspire you to search your soul and find the nexus between your passion and a paycheck so that you can live your life more abundantly.

Abundance is defined in the Merriam-Webster Dictionary as: 1. An ample quantity; 2. Affluence or wealth; and 3. A relative degree of plentifulness. When thinking of abundance, it is tempting to focus on money or material possessions as the primary markers of abundance. However, when I think of ample quantity, wealth, and plentifulness, it goes so much deeper than "things." It's about true love, pure joy, and a richness of spirit.

I grew up in an affluent community in the suburbs of Washington, D.C., where daily I encountered many "materially wealthy" people who were "poor in spirit." My favorite pastime was observing the antics of politicians, doctors, lawyers, and bankers who had massive homes, expensive cars, and flashy apparel, but often appeared empty inside. I didn't realize at the time that my ability to see that loneliness, brokenness, and longing for connection in people, from an early age, was directly linked to my purpose and how I am supposed to fully show up in the world. I've always had a "heart for people" and as early as the first grade, I exhibited emotional intelligence and a capacity to love, far beyond my young years. I was fortunate to grow up in an environment where adults encouraged me to find and use my voice, through chorus, theater, debate team, and more. I was blessed with the ability to explore my interests and cultivate my talents. I grew up believing there were abundant opportunities to be and have whatever I wanted in this world and the career possibilities were limitless. This made it difficult for me to distill my skills and talents to one career pursuit, as a child.

Every year I looked forward to career day at school, and showed up in a different costume like Halloween. One year I took my dad's old briefcase and wore a children's skirt suit, declaring that I wanted to be a real estate broker, just like him. The next year I wore my mom's scrubs and lab jacket and declared that I wanted to be a medical professional like her. The following year, I wore a makeshift robe and said I wanted to be a preacher. And my final year, I dusted off that old briefcase of my dad's and declared I wanted to be a lawyer when I grew up! This resonated with my parents, as I frequently exhibited traits that people associate with lawyers. I was a voracious reader, writer, and public speaker. I was always negotiating or advocating for my young rights and those of my peers. I once persuaded my whole class to sign a petition requesting the removal of a long-term substitute teacher after our original teacher fell ill and was no longer able to work while battling cancer. We had experienced so much trauma from losing our beloved teacher, who ultimately lost the battle, and I refused to add to that trauma by accepting an unkind substitute who lacked compassion for our circumstances. Once every student signed that petition and we submitted it to the administration, she was indeed replaced.

From the age of 12, I loved to dress up in little junior suits and I was always seen as mature for my age, so becoming a lawyer was a natural place to begin my pursuit in my journey to "abundance." My parents completely supported this goal and put a great deal of energy into helping me to reach it. They enrolled me in the Academy of Law program at my local high school and paid for me to participate in pre-law college preparatory summer programs. They supported me in participating in mock trial competitions and completing an internship with the Maryland state legislature. I had no shortage of support and belief in me achieving this goal and for that I was grateful, but I was never quite sure that becoming a lawyer was MY passion or my dream. Yet, being the people-pleaser that I was, I powered full steam ahead in pursuit of this goal that was laid out before me: to become the first lawyer in my family.

This secret doubt made my path to law school a winding road. I changed my major seven times in undergrad; yes, you read that correctly, SEVEN TIMES. The original major I declared when first accepted to Virginia Polytechnic Institute and State University (Virginia Tech) was English. I figured gaining a mastery of literature and writing would be a great gateway to a legal career, and in the worst-case scenario, I would be well-prepared for a number of professions, including education, journalism, and politics. It only took one semester for me to decide English was not the major for me! Too much red ink and subjectivity left me feeling like there were better ways to spend the four years, despite the "A" grade I received in my Freshman Honors English Course. The one class that stood out to me and really grabbed my attention that year was Sociology. I loved the science of understanding humans in relation to their broader societies and the socioeconomic impacts on specific communities within the global context. This ties back to my purpose which has always been to understand, advocate for, and serve others. I was so excited about my first Sociology class that I was convinced I wanted to shift my interests away from law school and go all the way up to a Ph.D. in Sociology. When I expressed this to my parents, they were less than enthusiastic about this shift in my interest. My father expressed that it was important to get my first degree in a field that could actually earn me a paycheck right out of undergrad and in his opinion, Sociology was not in that category.

I do not blame my father for his very limited view of what I needed to study in college to prepare me to earn a living wage, because he grew up in a time when the possibilities for a black woman in America were NOT limitless. When he met my mother in 1970s Brooklyn, New York, she believed that women had a choice of two types of work: Education or Healthcare. She was blessed enough to find her passion in that very limited paradigm as she was born to be a nurse! She attended an all-girls, vocational high school that prepared women for the nursing profession. She then attended college to receive her Bachelor of Science in Nursing and became a Registered Nurse. My mother worked as a nurse for over 40 years before retiring, and even now in retirement, she is called upon often to serve as a caretaker for family and friends recovering from illnesses and operations. She performs this work with passion and the highest level of care because it is what she was born to do and she has never wanted to do anything else. With her as my role model, throughout college, I set out on an endless pursuit to find that thing I could be passionate about, and I kept coming back to the social sciences. I finally settled on the seventh major because it was the one major I had enough credits in to graduate on time: Sociology & Anthropology with a focus on Criminal Justice/Pre-Law. So there I was, at the beginning of my Senior Year in undergrad, standing at the fork of my future with a choice of two roads to travel: A Master's Program for Social Work (MSW) or Law School. I think by now you might have an idea of what happened next in my story…

I started at Georgetown University Law Center in the Fall of 2004, after graduating from Towson University in the Spring of that same year. Law school was one of the most challenging times in my life, not just because it is hard for almost everyone, but because my heart was not in it. Several times in my cries for help, I prayed that family and friends would let me off the hook when I mentioned wanting to quit, but each time the refrain would be the same: "Law School is hard for everyone, you are smart, you can do it, and you will be the first lawyer in your family!" So I stuck with it, year after year, finding ways to make it more tolerable for myself. I shifted my focus to Education Law and Policy, joined the Students for Sensible Drug Policy, participated in Mock-Trial competitions, and helped to start a gospel choir at the school, that ended up singing the National Anthem at our commencement ceremony! I made the very best out of a difficult situation with the hopes of earning a hefty paycheck on the other side of the finish line! Well, of course, it wasn't that easy. When you are not passionate about something it shows. You may be able to skate along as long as no one is paying attention, but if people look closely enough, they see that you are not the right fit for roles that do not activate your passion.

Through a winding journey after graduating from law school in 2007, many legal career opportunities, and a mixture of other jobs in between, I took the first step on my journey to activating my passion, when I accepted a position in Human Capital. I worked my way up to Organizational Effectiveness where I was able to tap into my love for people in thinking about the "Humans" in our organization and what needed to be put in place to improve the employee experience. This work pulled on all the levers of my passion but also pulled on my sanity, being understaffed, under-resourced, and underappreciated at the organization. So ten years later, in 2014, I reached another fork in the road, once again with a choice to make that would determine what the next decade held in store for me. I left my job without another lined up, moved my family to Orlando, Florida, to be closer to my extended family, and took the opportunity to regroup and decide how I would proceed with my career. Was I going to double back and pursue a legal career again, despite how miserable the thought of that made me? Was I going to double down in this Human Capital career and continue to grow the skillset I had recently acquired, or was I going to take a leap of faith and go back to school to get my MSW to become a licensed clinical social worker (LCSW); a dream that I had deferred 10 years before when deciding to go to Law School?

As you probably guessed, I chickened out again and pursued a career that combined my legal and human capital backgrounds and joined a political lobbying organization as a public speaker, trainer, and member relations ambassador. I was able to flex and grow many of my skills, just as I did in my previous Human Capital career, and I worked with amazing people. I WAS very passionate about this work, but there were elements of it that always held me back from showing up authentically, and truly being able to help others in the ways I saw a clear need. I found myself acting as an unofficial therapist for both my colleagues and my clients, so often, that it sometimes interfered with my actual duties. I was told by many of my friends and former law school classmates that the work I was doing for this organization fell into the category of consulting, and I needed to work for a reputable firm to be compensated in a way that I deserved for my credentials and experience. After years of working with this organization, and understanding the needs of Florida's communities through the eyes of lawmakers and municipal leaders, I was ready to take my career to the next level with a reputable consulting firm.

For the first time in my life, I finally made it to PAYCHECKS! The money that my family and friends had hoped that I would make upon graduating from law school, I was finally making 15 years later. All the hard work, all the forks in the road, and all the life experiences were finally culminating in me gaining the fancy job, driving the luxury car, and finally actualizing the dream that so many had for me from young, yet I kept having this gnawing feeling that I wasn't fully living in my purpose. I didn't feel abundant even though I had more money and could travel the world, like never before! And it finally happened…

I couldn't run from my purpose anymore when I reached that fork again, almost 20 years from the time I decided to pursue law school over the option where my passion would be activated and sustained for years to come. In 2023, my family was hit with some major storms that would have devastated most families. When I felt like we finally hit rock bottom, I cried out to God this time, not friends or family, for guidance on how to get up. After months of crying out, one day I felt such an indescribable peace in that darkness and a light to guide me through, and out of it. I promised God I would stand firm in my convictions and my commitment to my family, and God promised me that I would never be forsaken but that I would be kept amid every storm to come. In this life, the only certain thing is that storms WILL rage against us whether pursuing our passions or completely off course. The rain doesn't fall on one man's house and we are all subject to be caught in the path of the storm. However, having faith in something greater than myself to get through it, gave me the strength to harness a limitless capacity for love, acceptance, understanding, and strength, and only then was I ready to go the other way at the fork in the road.

While I was getting to the other side of that proverbial storm, my husband and I decided to go to the movies one night, during an actual storm! It was pouring down, but it was date night, so we put on our rain jackets and headed out for the blockbuster film. As we were walking out at the end of the film, I received a text from one of my dearest old law school buddies that stopped me in my tracks, causing me to pause in a way that made my husband think someone had died! What was actually dying at that moment was the "old" me! The fearful me that longed for the approval of my family and friends; the me that always took the safe, sensible path; the me that was dissatisfied with the current state of my life because I was not fully showing up in it, but was too scared to do anything about it! What I'm describing was the "me" that went into the movie theater but not the same "me" that came out. The text from my good friend, whom I know to be a very spiritual woman who has never steered me wrong, read as follows:

"God told me to tell you it is time! It's time to walk in your purpose! Whatever it is, no matter how crazy it may seem to change course now, ask God for it and it will be granted unto you. This is a time for bold, wild faith to make a difference in this hurting world. Fear not, just ask!"

As I read these words, I felt a chill go up my spine! I felt my entire body radiating! I knew exactly what I wanted to ask God for and I knew that it was time to activate my passion! When we walked out of that theater, the storm had passed, the sky was clear, and I emerged a new woman from that place. I knew "paycheck" wasn't enough for me to feel whole anymore, and I was ready to walk in my purpose. I explained to my husband what I read from my friend, and he nodded silently and contemplatively, in agreement. The next morning I woke up and said, "I'm going back to school to be a therapist!" Just days before my 41st birthday, 20 years since I pushed this plan to the side and chose to go to law school instead, I began looking up MSW programs to apply and enroll for the next semester.

My story does not end there, the good part is just getting started. After all these years, I began my studies as an MSW candidate this past spring and quickly realized that the program did not have the right focus and structure to help me reach my goals. Instead of ignoring my spirit and pushing through, as I had done in Law School so many years ago, this time, I listened to that feeling in the pit of my stomach and mustered up the courage to walk away. This was the lesson I needed to learn; for me, this was growth! This was me having an honest conversation with myself and choosing my well-being and the pursuit of my purpose over the disappointment of others. I did not have the strength to face the shame of walking away at 22 years old, but "42-year-old me" finally believed in myself enough to walk away from what did not serve me.

So, my journey continues, and I am still on the path to realizing my passion for helping others therapeutically and doing meaningful, rewarding work. The best thing that came out of pursuing this educational opportunity, besides the lesson I learned, is that it connected me to multiple social service agencies and non-profits in the area that serve the community in powerful ways. When I decided not to continue with school, I instead committed myself to spending the rest of the year volunteering my time and talents with these organizations, trusting that they would lead me to the next steps in my journey through hands-on, experiential learning. As I write these words, I recognize what a gift it is from the Creator to have the ways and means to pursue my passions in safe and controlled environments. I recognize that everything is happening in its perfect time, in line with the Creator's perfect will. I recognize that continuing on the path to paycheck was a valid option to pursue and I would not look down on anyone who pursues that option as a means of survival. But as sure as you are reading these words, I want you to know that there is more to this life than surviving and I want to see you abundantly thriving, being brave, pursuing your passions and having all your needs AND wants met. As I write, I understand that this second half of my life is dedicated to doing what I was placed on this earth to do, and regardless of the career opportunities ahead, everywhere that I go from here on out will be fertile soil for me to plant my feet and grow in one way or another. I am so excited about my journey, and I want you to be excited about yours!

I want you to know that it is NEVER too late to change course. My desire is for you to find the smallest ways, daily, to activate your passions. And finally, I want you to "fear not and just ask" for whatever you truly, deeply want out of this life. Take inventory of what you love to do and when you feel most alive. In reading these words, you have already taken the right first step and I'm sure you won't have to dig too deeply to define your passion. Do you know deep in your heart what moves you? I'm certain you do. And once you've said it aloud, all I ask is that you begin to manifest it and run steadily toward your dreams. Take a small step today; take a bigger step tomorrow! Make a U-turn if you get off course and go the wrong way! But whatever you do, just start to run in that direction and watch the Creator show up for you every step of the journey!

Shwanda T. Barnette, J.D.

Shwanda T. Barnette, J.D. is a Human Capital Consulting Manager. Previously, she served as the Assistant Liaison to the Florida Black Caucus of Local Elected Officials (FBC-LEO). Shwanda received her Juris Doctor from Georgetown University Law Center in 2007. Following a judicial clerkship and adjunct teaching at Georgetown Law, Shwanda enjoyed a successful career with the District of Columbia government in Program Development, Human Capital Management, and Organizational Development for the District of Columbia Public Schools. DC Public Schools Office of Human Capital is where she first began her work in Diversity, Equity, and Inclusion (DEI) as a Peer Equity Counselor. Following her time at DCPS, Shwanda joined the Florida League of Cities University Team in 2016. She brought her experience in the DEI space to her work, supporting cities by designing and facilitating customize training sessions for elected officials and municipal staff on Ethics, Policy, and Leadership through a Diversity, Equity, and Inclusion framework. In October 2018, Shwanda received a professional certificate in Diversity & Inclusion for Human Resources from Cornell University's School of Industrial and Labor Relations.

Chapter 4

So Long, Insecurity

By Patricia Bates

"Trust yourself. You know more than you think you do."

– Dr. Benjamin Spock

Faith

Born and raised in Georgetown, Guyana, our home was never a faith-based home. My family went to church at Easter and Christmas, and on those days, my sisters and I went to children's church. I enjoyed it, and I remember my mom telling my dad we should go more often, but it never happened.

I was 11 when we moved to New York, and there was a church in the neighborhood 100 feet from my house. My dad was annoyed that I went there and told me it was only to meet boys. Little did he know the boys that went there were all from good wholesome families, and we would be lucky to associate with them. Much to my dad's annoyance, so many of the churchgoers were nice and neighborly. Clearly, church was not a part of his childhood although he died a devout Christian giving to many charitable organizations.

After I was married, we had our son christened in a Baptist church. Not only did my dad not come, but he also told all his friends not to go to the church because we would be there the entire day. They did, however, all come to the home celebration. How could you possibly miss your first grandchild's christening? These events were hurtful but I'm glad as the years went on things changed.

I enjoyed church so much, and learning to trust and have faith in the Lord in the early years of my marriage was key. We had bought our first home, and before the first mortgage payment, my husband, Eddie, broke his foot, and I lost my job. It was prayer and faith that kept us lifted. As years went by, and we moved from state to state, I always went to the yellow pages first to look for a church. When we left Florida to move to Georgia, I remember asking my pastor for recommendations for a new church.

Eddie, my husband, was not in tune with my love for church; however, I continued attending alone. He grew up in church and had gotten tired of going and being around pastors who were deceitful. I had no experience with any of that. I enjoyed visiting other churches and going to gospel concerts with my friends. The more I received, the more I wanted. I bought a "Good News" Bible so I could clearly understand the Word of God. I was baptized at the age of 27, and my son, Edward, was christened three months after his birth.

As I grew older, I felt the desire to learn and understand more. I decided to go back to school to learn the stories of the Bible in depth. I received my degree, and through all my studying, I felt a sense of calm and living more and more in my faith. I'm so grateful

I've been able to journal daily and been in prayer and praise to God. I've grown so much both from my schooling and practical knowledge. I love Christian music—gospel more than anything else. There is no greater peace than to know you can count on the One who is invisible and is always by your side. I am honored to be asked to publish this chapter in the *Bounce Back* book series.

Finances

Money in, money out—that was my childhood life. I watched my dad work two jobs to take care of us in a brand-new country where none of us knew the expectations. My mom stayed home until my brother was in kindergarten. I remember we were out shopping at a little boutique one day, and as we were walking home, we passed a store that had a "help wanted" sign. My mom did not drive, so this was the perfect location within walking distance of our home. She was hired, and independence overtook her. She quickly had her own money, credit cards, and not long after, enrolled in driving classes, followed by her first car purchase. She went to correspondence school for interior decorating and soon was promoted to manager of home furnishings.

My home was changed after my mom started working. I took on more household responsibilities and prepared dinner to help my mom.

For years, I was like my dad, being irresponsible with money. We never had conversations around financial responsibility or tithing in our home. Eventually, it was seeing the disappointment in my husband's face that led me to make a change in my ways. I wanted peace in our home and never wanted to fight over money. After all, it was just money—it comes, and it goes. It took years for me to learn to respect money as something God allows us to have to take care of our daily needs.

I am so thankful and grateful that the Lord has allowed me to save money over time. I have come to realize all my spending was satisfying my wants and not my needs, thus resulting in a lot of waste. I've developed a greater respect for money, which in turn, has created a more peaceful environment at home. I am out of credit card debt and on my way to paying off student loans.

Fitness

Growing up, I was known as "Fatty Patty." This nickname stayed with me until age 11, when I supposedly lost my baby fat. From then on, the only time I heard the name was when my cousins or my nanny came to see us, and the old days would come back. I was fit and trim growing up, and I even entered a beauty pageant once where I came in third place. My weight became an issue after Edward was born. Although I only gained 19 pounds, postpartum depression hit me like a boulder. I stayed in bed for days, was always emotional, and had no idea I was depressed. Finally, I changed jobs and started feeling better, but it was short lived. All my life I recall being on some type of diet—Think Thin in the 80s, Weight Watchers in the 90s, and anything else that came along. I always hated how I looked unless I was in a size 10.

As the years passed, and challenges, such as financial strains, arose in my home life, I turned to food to cope. Things I had never eaten before attracted me, and I began to feel out of control. It was a cycle—trying to feel better every day but not feeling better until I looked better—a real struggle! Being thin is a big deal for me, as my mother always criticized my weight. She wanted me to be married in a size 10 wedding dress and embarrassed me when the wedding gown was a size 14. I was a gorgeous bride, but all she saw was my weight.

In a town hall meeting one day, the new VP from Maine brought a freezer full of Ben and Jerry's ice cream. I had never heard of this ice cream before, but I tried it and could not believe how good it was. This was in 2001—I would eat a pint at a time all by myself. I started the South Beach Diet with Eddie in 2003, and I was so pleased with myself. Life was good again because I looked good, and the compliments were flowing for years.

In 2004, my marriage hit a low point, due to God knows what. People said it was a midlife crisis, but I only knew I wanted to be in my bed, totally alone. I lost my job and resorted to a diet of ice cream. It took years of therapy and staying away from negative family talk to get me back to some sense of normal. I was determined that "Fatty Patty" would leave forever, but she always came back.

I prayed and walked and prayed and ate sensibly. Eddie was supportive, and that was all I needed. I'm so thankful God gave me the grace and strength to walk daily and be able to lose 20 pounds that year. I was disciplined and devoted to my lean body system and healthy eating. I was amazed that I had no urges for fried food or Ben and Jerry's ice cream. I've always struggled, but this push paid off.

Family

Growing up, my parents never supported extracurricular activities. It was expected that my grades would be good, so much so that my parents never even checked my report card. It could have had all Fs, and no one would have known; however, it did not. In ninth grade, I failed math and science on purpose to see what would happen. No call went to the home, and only the bad grades showed up on the report card that was never seen. I was so frustrated. I might as well have been alone on an island. I would even leave my report cards with all As in the living room when I knew family was coming over, yet they were never noticed or spoken about.

The only way to gain visibility in my home was to clean the house. My dad would be so pleased but never said "thank you" or acknowledged it. He would whisper to my mom, "Why did she do that? What does she want?" The cleaning gained me new books from my mom, which I relished in. Therefore, whenever I needed a new dress or a new book, I was the best cleaner. Once, I even cleaned the shower doors with a toothbrush. Our home was 4,000 square feet, so it was a lot of cleaning.

Once married, Eddie and I shared everything. He cleaned better than I ever could. He also taught Edward to be able to do things on this own and not have to rely on a woman to cook, clean, and do laundry. I always wondered who raised Edward because he was such a fine young man. We would receive compliments about his kindness from neighbors all the time. I was proud, but surprised, knowing this was the child who ran the dishwasher several times so as not have to empty it! He worked in the church, and at times, would drive his dad to church. One Sunday, to my surprise, Eddie was outside helping Edward with the parking crew—this pleased me.

Edward was a great athlete and everyone recruited him for sports. He joined the band in middle school and played the clarinet as a first chair. We were so proud, but he hated it. Since we were paying for the clarinet, he could not quit. I also always wanted him to know that it was important to finish everything he started. He played baseball, ran track in high school, and was recruited for football and soccer. He joined the Reserve Officers' Training Corps (ROTC) but quit due to peer pressure that came from unwanted jokes about his uniform.

Edward started college and received all As his first semester. The day he decided to join the army I was literally in shock. We went to see the bus leave for the hotel they would stay overnight and I tried to stop the bus. I told the colonel that Edward could not go as he was my only son. The colonel advised me that Edward was not drafted, but that he volunteered. Edward thrived in the army, from basic training on. At graduation, he was selected to come out first and carry the flag for the entire battalion. He never told us in advance, and I was so proud.

From his first deployment to his eighth, Edward excelled and now leads the teams selected for the deployments. God has watched over him, and I am so grateful.

Although Edward was away an entire year on deployment, I was blessed with being able to see and talk to him while he was gone.

Of course, it is so good to have him permanently home this year to celebrate the holidays with us.

Fun

In my early adult life, I was introduced to network marketing, and I thought, "Finally, a way out!" I had made a dream board, and boy, did I dream. I worked, prospected, had home parties, and used the products, but then it fizzled out. Our upline was killed in a plane crash, and none of us kept in touch with the rest of the family. I kept going because my three prospects had already quit, and I never intended to quit. However, unfortunately one day, my dad, who prospected me, quit and never told me.

Many years later, I was introduced to the company Modere by one of my husband's former co-workers. I took off educating myself, finding out the nitty gritty (because I need to know everything about everything) and deciding to undertake a new endeavor. Business building was slow. I'd always been told I could sell swamp land, so I looked at the selling side with encouragement from my mentor. On Black Friday of my second year, I made it to the silver level and almost gold, in terms of sales, but never any further.

This year promises to be my finest year yet! Eddie and I have already planned two trips: one for Edward's homecoming and one for a family reunion where we'll see cousins we have not seen in years. We are thrilled at the opportunity to have fun without compromise. I've spent my life surrounding myself with people who made me feel less than, from childhood to adulthood. Finally, in my 67th year of life, I feel that I'm free to say, "So long, insecurity." Living life to the fullest has begun!

Patricia Bates

Hailing from Georgetown, Guyana, and raised in Long Island, New York, **Patricia Bates** is a dedicated dreamer at heart. Currently residing in Oviedo, Florida, she shares her life with her husband, Eddie, and their beloved Belgian Malinois, Maxwell. Her son, Staff Sergeant Edward Bates, serves overseas in the United States Army, while her brother and sister also call central Florida their home.

After graduating from high school, Patricia initially pursued a degree in marketing and management. However, her career path has led her on a 42-year journey in the health insurance industry, encompassing roles in insurance companies, startups, and esteemed organizations like Publix and Advent Health. Driven by her faith, Patricia delved into theology studies at Grand Canyon University, obtaining a bachelor's degree in biblical studies and a master's certification in youth and family ministries. The alignment between her role at Advent Health and her theological studies exemplifies a perfect fusion of her professional and personal passions.

Chapter 5

Life Is Like Climbing a Mountain

By James Bruce Sr., Ph.D.

"Faith is taking the first step even when you don't see the whole staircase."

— Martin Luther King, Jr.

When given the opportunity to contribute to a book about personal growth and overcoming obstacles, it seemed only fitting that I share from a perspective I am most passionate about. The following is an excerpt from my own book, *Life Is Like Climbing a Mountain*....

Can you remember the last time someone sarcastically told you to "take a hike"? Perhaps you were offended, and if so, good for you and more power to them. You received what you allowed, and you actually empowered that person by granting them control over your feelings and emotions. No doubt that person intended to be insulting to you. Perhaps their order to you was hurtful because you have not yet read this book, but of course you could not have read this book since it was not yet written. Okay, let us let the past be the past. From this point forward, though, if someone thinks they can offend you by telling you to "take a hike," respond by saying thank you and inform them that you are engaged in one right now or you were just thinking about taking one. You can explain to them that "taking a hike" is a high-level exploration whereby you are exercising your virtual mountain climbing skills. So, you will no longer be offended by an order to "take a hike," but instead, you will be encouraged to explore, believe, and achieve.

During and after your virtual mountain climbing excursion, you will be prompted to assess your personal character qualities during and after having emerged through the virtual mountain climb venture. Before beginning your journey, you must recite and believe these most powerful words: I can, I will, and it will happen. The objective of this book is to inform, educate, inspire, and motivate individuals and groups towards understanding oneself and others through a literal or virtual mountain climbing experience. The aim is to introduce the reader to a literary journey that involves the process and the act of mountain climbing. This book brings recognition to literal mountains that could be comprised of rocks, trees, ice, snow, and dirt. A mountain could be made up of a combination of the five kinds just listed. A volcanic mountain should be added, as a living rock, to this list of literal mountains. The volatility inherent in a volcanic mountain parallels the vulnerability and the potential explosiveness that exists in the individual human experience, as well as within our local and world communities.

These literal or physical mountains are used as a metaphor to offer insight towards understanding the dynamics and the challenges that are involved in the process of climbing a virtual mountain. The mountain climbing process might become more meaningful to an explorer who climbs a virtual mountain that ultimately takes the form of realizing a goal, dream, or aspiration. This book explores the spiritual aspect of the physical mountain, particularly in how the physical mountain has been a reference place for some people who testify to having a life-changing experience.

Finally, this book provides a strategic working road map that will transform the reader into a dreamer, and then into an explorer, a believer, and finally, an achiever. The achiever, in retrospect, will be inspired to recall and then recite the most powerful words: I said I can, I know that I would, and I made it happen. This "mountain climbing model" is useful towards attaining individual, personal, or collective goals, set in areas such as education, business, wealth building, job or career development, marriage, political aspirations, geographical relocating, reestablishing oneself, raising children, leading or managing sports teams, hiring and managing a work force, or even for the military that strategizes to win wars. This "climbing a mountain model" can be used for creating a strategic map towards achieving other personal goals, such as writing a book, building a house from the ground up, or regaining physical or mental health. Similarly, for organizations, this "climbing a mountain model" can be used as a guide when setting an organization's growth plans in motion. The principles are the same.

Understanding the Virtual Mountain Climb

According to Funk and Wagnall's *New International Dictionary of the English Language*, ©1995, the meaning of the word "challenge," amongst others, includes: "to invite or defy." These terms are the terms on which this book is postured. In other words, one is invited to climb a mountain, literally or figuratively, as in maneuvering through life with a determination to defy the obstacles and threats that come with the experiences. According to the same dictionary, the term "defy" means: "to resist successfully." For this chapter, this definition will be expressed in terms of resisting the thought of "failure" and declaring "victory" according to one's personal or organizational aspirations and achievements.

While climbing a real mountain, as well as living life, one should expect sudden changes of events to occur. Life challenges, or virtual mountains, are simply natural parts of life. Some obstacles will come with warning, while other challenges will just seem to appear. Unexpected changes will often require an entirely new set of workable plans in order to advance. A well-traveled path on a mountain might become suddenly interrupted as a result of a huge collapsed tree that has impeded the mountain climber's trail. The mountain climber might instantly require an alternative trail in order to continue the climb. A couple to be married might feel that a huge tree has crashed their wedding plans when the limousine that was scheduled for a 2 p.m. pick up will not be arriving.

In these two examples, the facts are clear that the huge tree has fallen and interrupted the mountain climb, and the limousine will not be taking the couple to the wedding ceremony. The challenge, or virtual mountain, in these two examples produces the question: What can or will be done by the actors in order to move forward?

Should the mountain climber, who is so determined to reach the top of the mountain, turn around and go home, or should the climber seek an alternative trail? Of course, the mountain climber should assess the feasibility of going over, under, or around the tree. The climber might consider a plan to backtrack down the mountain until an alternative trail to the top can be successfully traveled. For the couple to be married, should they cancel the wedding just because the limousine did not show up? Of course not. They should, like the mountain climber, assess the feasibility of the other alternatives towards declaring victory. For instance, they could use their personal vehicle, they could phone a friend, or they could even call for a taxi. In this case, the goal is greater than the means.

Each of the challenges, bouts, thrills, or experiences will need to be approached with the mastery of skills or appropriate tools that will make the mountain climbing experience more pleasant and achievable. Now, some of these skills will be natural, or previously attained (based on prior exposure), while other skills must be acquired, learned, and then mastered. Some of the tools can be self-managed, while some tools will require the assistance, guidance, and/or cooperation of others.

What Is Your Mountain?

Here are ten tips that may help you navigate through tough times:

1. ***Stay Positive***

    Maintain a positive attitude and believe in your ability to overcome challenges. Positive thinking can help you see the silver lining in difficult situations.

2. **Set Realistic Goals**

   Break down your challenges into smaller, manageable goals. Focus on taking one step at a time rather than feeling overwhelmed by the big picture.

3. **Seek Support**

   Don't be afraid to lean on friends, family, or a support group for help and guidance. Talking to others can provide perspective and emotional support.

4. **Take Care of Yourself**

   Make self-care a priority. Ensure you are getting enough rest, eating healthy, exercising, and engaging in activities that bring you joy and relaxation.

5. **Learn from Failure**

   View setbacks as opportunities for growth and learning. Reflect on what went wrong, adjust your approach, and keep moving forward with this newfound knowledge.

6. **Stay Flexible**

   Be open to adapting your plans and strategies as needed. Life is unpredictable, and flexibility can help you navigate unexpected challenges more effectively.

7. **Practice Mindfulness**

   Stay present in the moment and cultivate mindfulness through practices like meditation or deep breathing. Mindfulness can help reduce stress and improve your ability to cope with challenges.

8. ***Focus on Solutions***

   Instead of dwelling on problems, shift your focus to finding solutions. Brainstorm potential ways to address the challenge and take action towards resolving it.

9. ***Celebrate Small Wins***

   Acknowledge and celebrate even small victories along the way. Recognizing your progress, no matter how small, can boost your motivation and confidence.

10. ***Keep a Growth Mindset***

    Embrace a growth mindset, believing that you can improve and develop skills to overcome challenges. Approach obstacles as opportunities for personal growth and development.

Read more in my book, **Life Is Like Climbing a Mountain**, which is available in all bookstores.

James Bruce Sr., Ph.D.

Dr. James Edward Bruce, Sr. is a native Bostonian who has a genuine passion for teaching and writing. Each of his more than 50 published books are centered around motivational, educational, inspirational, and spiritual themes. Dr. Bruce encourages people to share what they know and give what they have while simply making room to receive those new blessings that are bestowed upon every individual at the dawning of each day. In his bestselling book, *Life Is Like Climbing a Mountain*, Dr. Bruce explores the spiritual aspect of the physical mountain as well as life parallels that we face each day.

Website: www.jamesbrucebooks.com

Chapter 6

Rock Your Shine After You've Been Cracked Wide Open

By Susan E. Casey, MSW, MFA

"Do not wait for someone else to come and speak for you. It's you who can change the world."

– Malala Yousafzai

On Valentine's Day in 2014, my 43-year-old brother Rocky (Brian) died from a brain infection in a hospital in Hong Kong. From the moment I received a call from his wife who said, "You have to be strong, Sue, Brian is gone," I felt as if God had reached down and pinched the sun like a candle flame and extinguished the light from my life. Hurtled into nowhere land, I had psychologically left the land of the living. Throughout the next several weeks, I was numb while going through the motions of writing his obituary, flying to Hong Kong with my older brother to meet my sister-in-law and 3-year-old niece, and taking care of endless red tape until we could get my brother's body released and cremated. After 10 days of feeling trapped in an altered reality, we collected my brother's bag of ashes and flew them back to Bali where he endured another two weeks of Hindu rituals to support my Balinese sister-in-law. There are no words in the English dictionary to adequately describe that experience of pure heartache. It's like sticking one's hand in a pool and trying to point out water—there is nowhere that grief doesn't leak into—it's everywhere.

I had never felt so detached from myself and others. I was terrified because I had no idea what to do or how to care about living. I was a therapist. I was supposed to know. Although I kept repeating the same narrative to myself, "This is temporary. It's going to be okay," it certainly didn't feel like it. My nicknames in high school were "Happy Hathaway" and "Susie Sunshine." The fear-based questions that crawled around my mind were: *What if I couldn't find my way back? What if I never felt joy again? What if I never trusted life again?* My fears were compounded by the gremlins scurrying from the corners of my mind, holding me hostage and prolonging my intense suffering from the insidious guilt I felt over things I did, things I didn't do, things I should have done, and things I could have done.

In the depths of my grief, I had forgotten something I believed deeply: Everything that happens to us, happens for us. When tragedy knocks on our door as it did for me, it's easy to forget this one universal truth. In hindsight, we often understand why things unfolded as they did. Imagine if we tapped into this wisdom during challenging times, trusting that all is happening for the higher good. Our suffering would be less intense and last for a shorter duration.

Experiencing the death of a loved one, a devastating divorce, or sudden job loss can throw us into an existential crisis, altering our perceptions. When crisis hits, our first reaction is often, "What did I do to deserve this?" or "What did I do wrong?" This mindset can plunge us into despair and anxiety or propel us into a profound spiritual awakening. Despair offers an opportunity to walk through the portal of grief and discover deeper meaning and joy.

As a psychic intuitive therapist, my clients do not come to me because they're sad over their loss. Sadness, grief, and mourning are all normal responses to loss. People seek out counseling to cope with what the trauma stirs up from the shadows that they grapple with, like shame and guilt from complex family dynamics. Another contributing factor that can prolong their suffering is their unwillingness to accept whatever tragic life event they are dealing with, especially when it's sudden, and they feel "blindsided" by it like I was with the death of my brother. We all have a choice when we are faced with adverse life events; we can move through them, run from them, or suppress them. I recommend that we move through them because we can't outrun them, and if we suppress those emotions, they will manifest into a physical or mental illness, or sometimes both.

Long before my brother's death, I wrote my dissertation on the healing benefits of writing through grief, loss, and trauma. A few months after Rocky transitioned, when I thought I couldn't tolerate one more moment of pain, I decided I had to help myself in all the ways I knew how: I stopped drinking and started writing. It took me four years to write my book from the time of inception to publishing, and in those four years, Rocky died over and over again. I allowed myself the space and the grace for my grief without judgment. I also surrounded myself with help. I saw a therapist and an energy worker and became a bereavement group facilitator. In the depths of the darkest period of my life and my journey back to the living, I found the deeper meaning of our existence and understood all the things I'd been studying for decades about life, death, and our purpose.

We are not here to judge ourselves or each other; we are here to accept and love ourselves and experience joy. We learn about love through connection to who and what brings joy into our lives. As we choose experiences that satisfy us, we lift our vibration and emanate more love and light into the world. We are powerful creators, and we are always contributing to the world through our thoughts.

Our thoughts create feelings, and our feelings create our vibrations. What do I mean by vibrations? Our bodies are made up of molecules vibrating constantly, creating electromagnetic waves, or what we call our "frequency." This is the vibe we send out to the world. Many people have heard about chakras, the main energy centers along our spine that contribute to our aura. These frequencies can be thought of as music we play in life's grand orchestra, shaping our experiences.

When we face tough emotions like grief, it's crucial to let ourselves fully feel them. If we don't, those emotions can get stuck and disrupt our frequency, affecting our physical and mental health. Our vibration emanates into the world and gets mirrored back to us through our experiences that show up in physical form. Many are familiar with the term "manifestation." What we manifest is a direct result of our vibration and our vibration is based on our alignment with love, which is our essence. At all times, we are either in alignment or out of alignment, and we can be in alignment in one area of our life and out of alignment in another. How do we know? By how we feel.

I hear young people nowadays talking about whether or not they "vibe" with someone. It's about feeling in sync, something that's become a big part of our pop culture dialogue, partly thanks to ideas popularized by the movie *The Secret*. We are beginning to have a much better understanding of how the energy we emit calls in our experiences and shows us the wounds we hold that need healing. When we are joyful, content, and at peace, our human self is aligned with our higher self/soul/source/God. The longer we remain in a joyful/satisfied vibration, the more experiences we call into our lives that perpetuate the peaceful feeling. The same is true when we hold the lower vibration of despair, hopelessness, and deep grief, which is why we feel so disconnected from ourselves and others. The longer we hold the in-alignment or out-of-alignment vibration, the louder it becomes. If you want to know how you're doing with your alignment to love, just look around at what is showing up in your life.

After Rocky died, I wanted to hibernate and shield myself from other people's energy. When I was around someone joyful, I felt irritated, and this was an indicator that I needed help to work through the intensity of the pain. The more I isolated, the more disconnected I felt from myself and others. We are pickers and choosers of our experiences—this is key to understanding how to become a screen where we allow our dense emotions of anger, grief, guilt, and shame to move through us rather than becoming the negative experience and staying in a density of low vibrational emotions.

What we focus on expands, which is why it is so crucial that we move dark energy and transmute it into light. This is especially critical when it comes to our rage. Many of us can feel intense rage following a devastating life event. I see this often with murder or deep betrayal in relationships. When we hang on to rage, we emanate a vibration of rage, creating more of what we don't want in the world. Does this mean we can magically stop feeling anger? No. It means it's important to feel it—not by screaming at people or through self-deprecation or self-injurious behavior—but through kindness and grace for oneself and through healthy and safe outlets, such as therapy, exercise, writing, praying, screaming, hitting a pillow, or any other outlet that will offer some release and relief.

As human beings, we make choices from moment to moment that will make us feel good, satisfy our desires, and bring us comfort and joy. We choose everything from our clothes, friends, and hobbies to our work, music, home, vacations, and more. We seek experiences that uplift, satisfy, and please us. Why, then, do we hang on to negative emotions and revisit the unpleasant experiences by replaying them in our heads? We get stuck in grief, anger, despair, or negative feelings for all sorts of reasons; we tell ourselves a story, and we begin to believe that narrative. We feel justified in holding on to rage over infidelity, for example.

When we choose to become the negative experience rather than use it to show us our preference, like finding a loyal and loving partner, we torture ourselves and compound and prolong our suffering, believing we are victims rather than the creators of our lives. When we hold on to rage, it does not impact the person who angered us; it only hurts and steals our peace and joy. Would a vegetarian walk into a restaurant and order a steak? Would someone allergic to wool walk into a clothing store and buy a wool sweater? Would a person buy a pair of shoes two sizes too small? Would a music enthusiast make a playlist of songs they hate? Of course not. We never willingly choose things that make us feel crappy, and yet, we'll hang on to unpleasant emotions for a lifetime or stay in dissatisfying relationships for decades.

Why would we do this? So often we do not understand we have a choice as to how we feel. If we don't like the song on the radio, what do we do? We change the station. The same is true for our thoughts. If you don't like your thoughts, change them; shift your focus to what makes you feel good. If you're miserable in your relationship, understand the root and either change it to get into alignment with it or move on. And if you're grieving a loss of any kind, feel it, move it, lean into what brings you comfort, and do this every time that wave pulls you under until your heart has healed.

We will always have contrast because we can only create what we want by understanding what we don't want, and that understanding comes from our experiences. We are here to shine our divine spark. The name of my company is *Rock Your Shine: After You've Been Cracked Wide Open* because, for so many of us, we find our passion in the deep contrast to it—that feeling of despair and disconnection that we feel in the throes of life's painful events.

What's your passion? Do you know? What breaks your heart? What makes you angry? Do the positive of what causes the heartbreak and anger. Do it with love and belief in yourself. Go rock your shine because it is what we are all born to do.

Susan E. Casey, MSW, MFA

Susan E. Casey, MSW, MFA, is an author, a licensed mental health clinician, a certified bereavement group facilitator, and a certified life coach. Throughout the past 25 years, Susan has worked in hospice, in-patient, and home-based settings with teens and adults and taught numerous courses to executive leaders and clinicians. Currently, Susan works for a measurement-based care organization, providing clinical coaching to therapists, psychologists, and psychiatrists countrywide to improve mental health outcomes for youth and adults. Susan also teaches an eight-week online grief and loss course for those who have lost a sibling.

Susan's blog on her website chronicles her grieving process following the death of her younger brother. *Rock On: Mining for Joy in the Deep River of Sibling Grief* was her first work of nonfiction, published on February 14, 2020, by Library Tales Publishing. *Rock On* won first place in the general nonfiction category of the Royal Dragonfly book contest and was a finalist in the Best 2020 Books American Fest national book contest and the Book Excellence national book contest. Her fiction has also won numerous awards, including first place in the PEN/Nob Hill Literary Contest and Green Writer's National Literary Contest. Both Susan's professional and creative work have been guided by her deep belief that every individual has purpose and inherent strengths and deserves the opportunity to reach their own unique potential. Susan lives in Maine with her husband, Steve, and mini Aussiedoodle, Rocky.

Email: rockyourshine@gmail.com

Website: www.rockyourshine.com

Chapter 7

Intentionality and Clarity for Positive Action

By Andy Charles

"Don't let the noise of other's opinions drown out your own inner voice."

- Steve Jobs

I have looked objectively at many of the great athletes and realized that they all have one thing in common: They all knew (and some continue to know) how to mentally bounce back and be resilient, and they displayed this most when their backs were up against a wall. I deeply admired that they displayed such mental discipline, and they were able to overcome what seemed impossible with sheer gut, courage, and determination. I speak highly of Michael Jordan, Kobe Bryant, Tiger Woods, Novak Djokovic, Lionel Messi, and Usain Bolt. I could go on and on, but by now, I hope you can see my observation—they all had challenges that were huge and intimidating to the average athlete, but these men proved the right mindset and conviction of heart can make the spirit excel where others might fail. Don't forget about Serena Williams, Elaine

Thompson, Dana Patrick, and Annika Sorenstam. I am sure by now the picture is getting clearer in your mind: Some phenomenal men and women have bridged the gap between failure and success and fear and dare and have left many examples of how we too can overcome if only we saw things differently in the pursuit of our dreams.

I remember listening to an interview with Kobe Bryant speaking about a career-threatening injury (his Achilles' tendon was torn) in a game against the Golden State Warriors. It required surgery, and he was 34 years old at the time. Somehow, Kobe managed to still make two free throws and, sometime later, he posted these words on his Facebook wall: "If you see me in a fight with a bear, pray for the bear." I've always loved that quote. That's "mamba mentality"—we don't quit, we don't cower, we don't run. We endure and conquer. What kind of mentality and pure heart does it take to see life from that perspective? For Kobe, it was not about the injury but what he would do about it. That same mindset caused Mike Tyson to say: "I have to dream and reach for the stars, and if I miss a star then I grab a handful of clouds." God lets everything happen for a reason. It's all a learning process, and you go from one level to another.

> *As long we persevere and endure, we can get anything we want.*
>
> —***Mike Tyson***

My biggest takeaway from these examples is that when we are willing to accept responsibility for the outcomes we desire, and we are willing to pay the price of that responsibility, we open a whole new world of possibilities that may not have existed before. Nothing is in its final stage in life unless it is dead, done and over with. You do not perform an autopsy on the living, so while there is still life to breathe, walk, and talk, you can also keep the dream alive.

How does one make a dream, or a vision, become a reality? Is there any specific technique or mindset one must have? Or is there just raw ambition, passion, and intentionality? These elements, when put together in the right environment, can be a technique. Additionally, the greatest achievers found a way to master their techniques, and in the process, became masters of themselves.

Self-mastery is not a condition of finality. It is, however, a condition of continuity—it never stops—and it allows one to show up in the world as the best version of oneself regularly. When I studied human and social psychology, we were told about seeing the world in "life positions." My favorite was: I am okay, you are okay. The reason why I liked this was because it meant I was willing to see people as myself. I was willing not to look at someone from a faulty or differently-abled position. I was willing to embrace anyone just as they were created and placed by the Creator for a purpose. Who was I then to see myself as being superior and they as being inferior? This just made sense. I did not need the tenets of religion to come to this conclusion—it was just decent human thinking and a desire to build relationships with people everywhere. I realized that the world is just one big community—a gigantic neighborhood of various races, creeds, and colors—and all of us were placed here to complement the lives of others.

This is everyone's true calling, and how we respond to this determines our ability to respond to life's responsibilities. One of our greatest responsibilities is to invest in ourselves to ensure that our dreams see the light of day. Too many are lying in their graves with the last thought of regret lingering eternally simply because they feared to dare, attempt, and try. Never wait until you think the time is right or the conditions are ideal—they may never be. Do not wait until you have enough zeros in your account or enough initials before and after your name. Start now right, where you are. Begin the process because tomorrow is never promised, and the time that matters the most is what you have right now. For the record, fear is an emotion that is as human as any other, but it can also be managed; the key to this management is based on the process of thought.

What we think determines what we feel, and how we respond or react to what we think determines how we feel. Therefore, if we are aware of the process of thought, then it automatically brings us a sense of awakening. This awakening leads us to ask ourselves questions about our thoughts. Always question the source of your thoughts, and if that source is not your choice, then open the door of your mind and show that to your thought.

You have the final say as to what stays in your mind, and by extension, what emotions are now being entertained. Give that power to no one, and take control of it without negotiation or compromise. A famous coach once said, "Many people wait around in life hoping that other people would build bridges for them to cross the canyons of their lives, but what many do not realize, is that within them lies the ability to grow wings and soar over the canyons of their lives." The ability to gain momentum in any given situation is something that can always prove to be one's advantage. Once the process has begun, you can't afford to stop. Slowing things down may become necessary from time to time, but the key to driving success and building dreams is to keep moving. It is better to make small steps of progress daily than to try and engage the entire project all at once. When you engage incrementally, it gives you the advantage of gauging progress while keeping the end goal in mind.

Maintaining focus is critical to enjoying the process and learning the discipline of overcoming fear. It is a vital ingredient in the cog of success and helps us to remember that the journey is the teacher, and by gaining the experience, we have become its students. The daily encounters of life, whether they be good, bad, or indifferent, are all classrooms of learning. The quality of the lessons we receive depends on the lens through which we see these lessons.

Life is never happening to us; it is always occurring for us. Every encounter has a diamond or two waiting to be discovered. Don't be afraid to imagine, and don't be afraid to dream. You can never tell when your imagination can become a preview of your destiny or a highlight of who you can become tomorrow. Always live in the anticipation that there is a better version of you somewhere in your future, and now is a time of preparation to meet that version soon. Look forward with hope to a brighter day and a better tomorrow. Visualize your best times being ahead of you and still in the making. Drive on with passion and belief that even though some tasks may be daunting, deep within you lies the ability to manage, overcome, and push on.

Giving up was and should never be an option. Leave no room for negative influence to enter the equation. The only thing that makes sense is the next step forward; even if you can't see where you are stepping, take a step of faith. Moving in the right direction with the right mindset can get you the right results. You may stumble because of the terrain or the absence of light, but that is no excuse to stop—it is time to move. You will never know what is behind the darkness until you get there, and you may never know what is around the corner until you make the turn. Always keep in mind that your dream is worth the effort, and at some point, you shall reap the benefits. Your journey is only over when you say it's over. Additionally, if you are spiritually connected like I am, remember the Scripture from 2 Timothy 1:7, which says, "For God hath not given us the spirit of fear, but of power, and of love, and of a sound mind." What do you choose? Godspeed.

Andy Charles

Andy Charles is an internationally certified life and development coach. He has been coaching for the past 15 years, and his accreditation comes from www.coaching.com and the International Coaching Federation (ICF). Andy holds an MBA certification in international business and is a certified public speaker and speechwriter from Udemy. He is also a security practitioner who owns a protective service agency, a minister of the Gospel, a transformational speaker for the past 20 years, a singer, a three-time podcast host, and a writer who has one published novel, entitled *To Lose a Dream,* and three eBooks on Amazon. As a member of Lions Clubs International, Andy was the awardee of a certificate of recognition for his work as a membership coordinator (team coaching) by the international president.

Andy's life statement is to have valuable family time on premium vacations, be a servant to his gifts, and a slave to his calling through God whilst building great relationships with people all over the world. His purpose is to inspire empowerment and transformation for people to live a life of fulfillment and resilience. His lifelong dream is to inspire transformation in over three million people during his lifetime. Andy is a husband, father of three, and grandfather of five. His hobbies are meeting people, music, and writing, and he loves the sport of golf.

Biosite Link: https://bio.site/andyspersonaldevelopment

Author Link: https://www.amazon.com/author/andycharles

Podcast Link: https://podcasts.apple.com/us/podcast/andy's-personal-development/id1577374724

Chapter 8
Rediscovering My Voice

By Mercy Chogugudza

"Fear imprisons, faith liberates; fear paralyzes, faith empowers; fear disheartens, faith encourages; fear sickens, faith heals; fear makes useless, faith also makes serviceable."

—Harry Emerson Fosdick

In life, we often find ourselves navigating between saying yes and saying no. There's a delicate balance between accommodating others and prioritizing our own needs. For a long time, I focused on learning to say no, setting boundaries, and understanding my limitations. While this was a crucial phase of growth, I eventually realized that there was more to my journey than just learning to decline. I embarked on a new chapter of self-discovery, one where I put myself first and embraced the essence of who I am. This journey of self-discovery wasn't just about learning to say no; it was about saying yes to myself. It involved rediscovering my passions, strengths, and values and aligning my life with them. It meant shedding old beliefs and expectations that no longer served me and embracing the freedom to define my own path. Through this process, I learned to trust my instincts, honor my intuition, and embrace the fullness of my being. It was a journey of empowerment, self-love, and authenticity.

Embracing Self-Discovery: Overcoming Guilt and Shame

The journey of self-discovery is not always straightforward. It involves delving into our past, understanding our values, and accepting our strengths and weaknesses. I had to understand my past to comprehend where I was heading. Growing up, my life coping skills were deeply rooted in a history of being a "yes-woman." I often put others' needs before my own, sacrificing my well-being in the process. This pattern led to a sense of fulfillment externally but left me hollow internally, lacking a true understanding of my own desires and aspirations.

Putting myself first meant acknowledging that my needs are just as important as anyone else's. It meant setting aside guilt and prioritizing self-care without apology. This shift in mindset was liberating and empowering. I discovered a newfound confidence in owning my decisions and embracing my authentic self. By understanding my values and aligning my actions with them, I found a deeper sense of purpose and fulfillment. This journey was about reclaiming my voice and identity, stepping into my power, and living life on my terms.

Accepting my strengths and weaknesses was a crucial part of this journey. I learned to celebrate my successes without downplaying them and to embrace my vulnerabilities as opportunities for growth. Self-acceptance allowed me to let go of unrealistic expectations and embrace a more compassionate view of myself. It was a journey of self-discovery and self-love, where every step forward was a reaffirmation of my worth and potential. This process continues to evolve, shaping my path with authenticity, resilience, and a deep sense of inner peace.

Letting Go of Guilt and Shame

Letting go of the guilt was not easy. There were moments I felt shame—shame that I was being this horrible person for making changes in my life. Negative things were also happening in my life, with illnesses and deaths occurring in my extended family. I began to believe that these events were punishments for the changes I was making. It felt like God was punishing me, and I found myself spending a lot of time in that guilt and shame space. I grieved a lot during this period, grieving the death of the old me. I didn't know the new me, and all I had was an idea of who she would be, but for a person like me who likes to be in control, it was tough and uncomfortable.

Another example of this struggle was in my professional life. As I moved up the corporate ladder, I encountered situations where I had to make tough decisions that affected people's livelihoods. I often carried the weight of these decisions with me, feeling guilty for any negative impact they might have had. It took time to realize that while empathy is important, I couldn't let guilt consume me. I learned to make decisions based on values and integrity, understanding that not every choice will please everyone but striving to do what's fair and ethical.

In relationships, letting go of guilt and shame meant setting boundaries and prioritizing my well-being. I used to feel guilty for saying no or asserting my needs, fearing that I might disappoint others. However, I came to understand that healthy boundaries are essential for healthy relationships. It was a process of learning to communicate effectively, express my feelings without guilt, and surround myself with people who respect and support me.

Additionally, letting go of societal expectations and embracing my authentic self was a significant part of releasing guilt and shame. Society often imposes unrealistic standards and labels that can make us feel inadequate or ashamed of who we are. Through self-discovery and self-acceptance, I learned to silence those external voices and define my own worth. This meant letting go of perfectionism, embracing my flaws, and understanding that growth comes from embracing our imperfections.

Navigating Fear of Change

Navigating the fear of change was a profound aspect of my self-discovery journey. I questioned if my spouse would love the new version of myself and if my children would still give me unconditional love. These doubts stemmed from a fear of rejection, a fear that my evolution might disrupt the dynamics of my closest relationships. I also grappled with my faith, wondering what God thought of this new person I was becoming. Would I still be accepted and loved by the divine, or would my changes lead to spiritual estrangement?

This period was marked by uncertainty and fear of the unknown. It was a struggle to confront these fears head-on and embrace the discomfort that comes with growth. I had to remind myself that change is a natural part of life, and stagnation often leads to discontentment. Embracing the unknown became a mantra, a way to open myself to new possibilities and experiences that aligned with my evolving self.

Trusting in the process was another crucial aspect of navigating fear of change. I had to believe that the changes I was making were for my highest good, even if they challenged my comfort zone. This meant letting go of the need for external validation and finding validation within myself. It was about honoring my journey and having faith that I was moving toward a more authentic and fulfilling life.

In the midst of these fears, I discovered resilience and inner strength. I learned to lean into discomfort, knowing that growth often emerges from moments of uncertainty. This mindset shift allowed me to embrace change as an opportunity for personal evolution rather than something to be feared. It was a transformative shift that propelled me forward on my journey of self-discovery and self-empowerment.

The Joy of Learning New Skills

The joy of learning new skills has been an exhilarating and transformative aspect of my journey. One of the most memorable moments was when I decided to learn how to ride a bike. While this may seem like a simple task for many, it held significant meaning for me. Despite having purchased bicycles for my children over the years, I had never taken the time to learn myself. The thought of balancing on two wheels and navigating the streets filled me with both excitement and apprehension.

I vividly remember the day I finally mustered up the courage to try. With shaky legs and a determined mindset, I set out to conquer this challenge. The initial wobbles and near falls were met with laughter and encouragement from my family. Each attempt brought me closer to mastering the art of balance. And then, in a moment of sheer determination, I felt it—the sensation of gliding forward, the wind in my hair, and a rush of freedom unlike anything I had experienced before. The joy I felt upon mastering this seemingly simple skill was indescribable. It wasn't just about riding a bike; it was about overcoming self-doubt, pushing past fears, and embracing a newfound sense of capability. It taught me the power of persistence and resilience, reminding me that growth often lies just beyond our comfort zones.

Similarly, learning to fly—both literally and metaphorically—was a remarkable experience that left a lasting impact on me. When my children surprised me with a ticket to an indoor skydiving facility, I was both excited and nervous. Stepping into the wind tunnel, I was met with a rush of adrenaline and a sense of weightlessness as I floated mid-air. It was a surreal experience that symbolized letting go of inhibitions and embracing the unknown.

The process of learning these new skills taught me valuable life lessons. It taught me that growth happens when we challenge ourselves, and it's okay to stumble and fall as long as we get back up and try again. It showed me the importance of perseverance, courage, and the sheer joy of pushing boundaries. These experiences of learning new skills became pivotal moments of empowerment and self-discovery on my journey, reminding me that the possibilities are endless when we open ourselves up to new experiences.

Returning to My Roots

Returning to my roots has been a deeply meaningful part of my journey. Having been raised in a religious family, I found myself drawn back to the core of my upbringing. Rediscovering my faith became a significant aspect of my self-discovery journey. It provided a sense of grounding and purpose, guiding me through life's uncertainties and offering solace during challenging times.

However, this journey back to my roots wasn't always straightforward. Along the way, I encountered temptations and distractions that tested my resolve. There were moments of doubt and questioning, where I grappled with reconciling my beliefs with the complexities of life. Yet, through these struggles, I found strength and clarity in my faith. It became a source of resilience, helping me navigate challenges with a renewed sense of purpose and perspective.

Returning to my religious roots also meant reconnecting with a community that shared similar values and beliefs. It provided a sense of belonging and support, fostering meaningful connections and deepening my understanding of spiritual principles. The rituals and practices of my faith became anchors in my daily life, reminding me of the importance of gratitude, compassion, and service to others.

This journey of returning to my roots has been profoundly fulfilling. It has allowed me to reconnect with a part of myself that I had temporarily set aside, finding peace and strength in the familiar embrace of my faith. It's a journey of ongoing growth and introspection, where I continue to deepen my spiritual connection and find meaning in the timeless wisdom of my religious heritage.

Navigating Pushback and Growth

Navigating pushback and growth has been a defining aspect of my journey. As I embraced self-discovery and returned to my religious roots, I encountered pushback from some quarters. People noticed my growth and evolution, and not everyone was supportive. Some attempted to guilt-trip me into abandoning my journey, questioning my choices and beliefs. Despite these challenges, I remained steadfast in my pursuit of self-empowerment and authenticity.

The pushback I faced taught me valuable lessons about resilience and staying true to myself. It forced me to confront external pressures and societal expectations, challenging me to define my own path. Instead of succumbing to guilt or doubt, I used these experiences as opportunities for growth and introspection. I learned to trust my instincts, honor my values, and embrace my unique journey, regardless of external opinions.

Navigating pushback also required me to cultivate a strong sense of self-confidence and self-worth. I realized that my worth isn't determined by the approval or validation of others. It comes from within, from honoring my truth and living authentically. This mindset shift empowered me to navigate challenges with grace and resilience, staying true to my beliefs while remaining open to growth and new perspectives.

Navigating pushback and growth became an integral part of my self-discovery journey. It taught me the importance of staying true to myself, even in the face of adversity. It reinforced the idea that embracing who we are meant to be often requires courage, resilience, and a steadfast commitment to our own growth and authenticity.

Reclaiming Your Voice

Rediscovering myself meant reclaiming my voice. It was about expressing my thoughts, opinions, and emotions authentically. No longer bound by fear or hesitation, I spoke up with confidence. I realized that my voice matters, and sharing my perspective contributes to meaningful conversations. Whether through writing, speaking, or simply engaging with others, I found empowerment in using my voice to make a difference.

The journey from learning to say no to rediscovering my voice and returning to my roots has been transformative. It's a continuous evolution of self-discovery, growth, and self-empowerment. Putting myself first doesn't mean being selfish; it means honoring my worth and embracing all that makes me unique. Through travel, quiet moments, returning to my religious roots, learning new skills like riding a bike and flying, and reclaiming my voice, I've learned that true fulfillment comes from living authentically and embracing the journey of becoming who I am meant to be.

I am thriving now, and I have no regrets. I am loving myself and others in a healthy way. The analogy of when you are on a plane, and they tell you to put on your mask first before you help others is so apt with my journey. I have learnt to breathe again—this time differently—this time in a healthy way. I love me!

My journey is a testament to the power of self-discovery and self-love. It's a reminder that no matter where we are in life, it's never too late to embrace change, reclaim our voice, and live authentically. Each step forward, no matter how small, has the potential to lead to profound transformation. I invite you to embark on your own journey of self-discovery, to embrace your uniqueness, and to love yourself unapologetically. You deserve to thrive, to be heard, and to live a life that reflects the true essence of who you are.

Mercy Chogugudza

Mercy Chogugudza is a dynamic and visionary leader in the field of human resources whose expertise and passion have transformed organizations and empowered individuals to reach their full potential. With a wealth of experience in designing, managing, and facilitating impactful leadership development programs, Mercy has become a trailblazer in creating cultures of collaboration and implementing change strategies that foster workforce excellence.

Mercy's extensive experience in human resources spans various areas, including organizational development, succession planning, and total rewards programs. Her coaching skills have led to significant achievements in transformational leadership, intercultural communication, team building, and change management. She is highly regarded for her ability to develop effective employee retention programs. Driven by a genuine love for people, Mercy embodies the human side of human resources. Her passion lies in bringing out the best in individuals by empowering them to reach their full potential. She lives by the mantra, "Be the change you want to see," inspiring others to embrace their unique talents and aspirations.

Beyond her professional endeavors, Mercy cherishes her role as a mother to two sons and a loving wife. In her leisure time, she finds solace in the great outdoors, immersing herself in nature's beauty and rejuvenating her spirit. She also channels her energy into engaging DIY projects, embracing creativity and personal growth in every endeavor she undertakes. Moreover, Mercy selflessly volunteers her time to organizations dedicated to empowering women and nurturing the well-being of children, further exemplifying her dedication to making a positive impact on society.

Mercy's remarkable journey as an HR knowledge leader and transformative professional is a testament to her unwavering commitment to excellence, her ability to foster collaboration, and her belief in the power of human potential. Her story is an inspiration to aspiring leaders and a testament to the profound impact one individual can have when driven by the mantra, "Be the change you want to see."

Chapter 9

Values and Boundaries

By Vanessa Ingrid Farrell

Do not conform to the pattern of this world, but be transformed by the renewing of your mind. Then you will be able to test and approve what God's will is—his good, pleasing and perfect will.

—Romans 12:2

I can relate to the struggle of losing sight of one's values and identity as a woman in the dating world. It is easy to enter a relationship with confidence, believing that I know exactly who I am. But then, unexpectedly, I find myself faced with a situation that forces me to choose between my prince and my principles. In those moments, my instincts scream at me to make a different choice—to stand up for myself or to leave. However, I often ignore my intuition, stay silent, and overstay my welcome.

Days later, as I gather my senses and regain my dignity, I am filled with horror and disbelief as I look at myself in the mirror. I try to reconcile what just happened and how easy it was to live a hijacked life, but it is often too late. Whether I have compromised my values to appease someone or tolerated repeated deception, I have found myself in those situations more times than I care to admit. In those moments of self-betrayal, I have made a promise to myself and to God that I will never allow any man to treat me that way again. However, to my disbelief, I have found myself repeating the same old patterns.

In those instances when I didn't feel like an equal in a relationship or when I was disrespected, I realized that it was because I had willingly handed over all my power or failed to use my voice. Despite knowing deep down that something was off, I still allowed myself to engage in those situations. I am in no way condoning such insults, but it wasn't solely the other person's fault; I also had a role to play in what happened. I could have chosen to walk away and protect myself and my sanity, but instead, I chose to stay and endure the nonsense. Upon reflection, I have realized that I needed to take responsibility for my own actions and choices.

Over the years, whenever a relationship ended, I would find myself in a state of introspection, analyzing every detail and trying to understand where things went wrong. Hoping to gain some clarity, I would even go as far as asking suitors for their perspective on the demise of our relationship. However, apart from them thinking I had lost it, their responses often fell short of satisfying my curiosity and didn't provide the closure I was seeking.

After realizing the pointlessness of my quest and the negative impact it had on my confidence, I decided to take a different approach to dating. Looking for clear answers, I embarked on a deeper exploration of biblical guidance on relationships. To my surprise, I discovered that the Bible does not explicitly address the concept of dating as we understand it today, and for a minute, I was left wondering if dating was even a biblical concept at all.

However, as I studied the Bible, I discovered a wealth of valuable principles and instructions that resonated with me and could be applied to relationships between men and women, including those in the context of dating. These principles include maintaining sexual integrity, seeking God's guidance in relationships, connecting with those who share similar faith and values, and fostering a mutual level of respect and selflessness. I expanded my understanding of relationships and dating by actively seeking wisdom, advice, and guidance from trusted friends and mentors. I wasn't shy about reaching out to them for their insights and experiences because they were the people I thought of as members of my trusted circle. Additionally, I journaled a lot and immersed myself in books, sermons, podcasts, and workshops that focused on relationships and dating.

Through my study, I stumbled upon Gary Chapman's book, *The Five Love Languages*. Though it is written for couples, I dug into this book with insatiable eagerness, and it became a game changer for me. The premise of the book is that understanding and speaking your partner's primary love language is essential for a fulfilling and lasting relationship. I found that these principles were applicable in fostering general friendship and in dating. I also found that attending singles ministries, workshops, and seminars provided valuable opportunities to learn from experts and engage in discussions with others who were also seeking growth in this area. Finally, I utilized the Internet as a resource, exploring many websites and even enrolling in a private virtual membership program that offered personal and group coaching, information, and perspectives on relationships.

I have reached a point in my life where I feel completely at ease expressing my values as a woman. It was a journey that required time and introspection as I sought answers to a series of challenging questions I developed from various sources throughout my learning process. The core questions included:

- What are the principles I firmly believe in and I will never compromise on?
- What qualities do I genuinely admire in others?
- What kind of person do I desire to be?
- What brings me real joy?
- What aspects of my life do I prioritize?

Answering these questions required deep soul-searching as I aimed to be honest and thoughtful in my responses. Through this process, I had the courage to identify and embrace faith, respect, honesty, health, generosity, gratitude, and wisdom as the core values that resonate with me on a profound level.

During this time of personal reflection, as I delved into the process of refining my values, I gained a newfound clarity regarding the importance of setting boundaries. It became evident that my values and boundaries are deeply intertwined, and one was the foundation on which the other stood. There were boundaries that I immediately knew had to be established and affirmed. They were as basic as requesting a courtesy phone call rather than having someone show up unannounced at my home to as courageous as letting suitors know I am on an abstinence journey, and I will not engage in sexual activity while dating. This was a giant step because in the past I had not been particularly good at establishing, stating, and maintaining boundaries in my dating relationships. It felt as though my boundaries were equivalent to drawing a line in the sand, only for them to gradually be washed away by the incoming tide. These tides were the small offenses that occurred over time, slowly eroding trust and stifling all hopes and desires for what the relationship could be.

Making the decision at the age of 42 to abstain from sex was more challenging to explain than it was to put into practice. Despite never allowing myself to be driven by sex or making it the focal point of my relationships, and instead taking the time to truly get to know the person I was dating, this approach often proved to be difficult to implement. It became clear that no amount of gathering information, vetting someone's character, or following the 90-day rule could guarantee success. The 90-day rule comes from the book *Act Like a Lady, Think Like a Man*. According to author Steve Harvey, the 90-day rule is the minimum amount of time that a woman should wait before becoming sexually intimate with a man. Harvey feels that this time gives both people the opportunity to get to know each other on a deeper level. Furthermore, it allows the woman to gauge the man's intention and possible commitment beyond the physical. These were solid instructions; however, it was not until I really assessed my own core values and beliefs that I was led to abandon my vague boundaries and establish a wall of sexual purity in my dating life.

Despite unwavering support from some people in my life, my decision was also met with skepticism and sarcasm from others. However, I remained determined. Men and women alike would often respond with comments like "good luck," implying that it was nearly impossible to achieve such self-control. Some would snap back with comments like, "Better you than me" or "I would just die," insinuating that I possessed a unique willpower that other women or men lacked. Others would cautiously ask, "So, what would you do when…," their voice trailing off as they struggled to find the right words. I would meet their gaze and inquire, "When…

what?" This forced them to confront their assumptions. They would then timidly ask, with a hint of a smirk, how I would handle sexual desires, as if they were a disease and sex was the only cure. With a straight face, I would add a touch of humor, letting them know I would simply take a cold shower and pray.

Seven years later, at the ripe old age of 49, I guess cold showers and prayer were no match for my fleshly desire when I found myself in a compromised place. I had broken my vow of abstinence and had had sex. On one hand, there was a sense of satisfaction and a renewed feeling of connection and intimacy with a potential partner; we had known each other for almost two years, and it felt like there was a possibility of a relationship. On the other hand, I couldn't shake the feelings of guilt, regret, and disappointment. I constantly questioned whether I had made the right decision and felt overwhelmed with guilt for abandoning my values and beliefs.

The internal conflict of breaking my commitment to abstinence weighed heavily on me, and I struggled for a long time to reconcile my actions with my personal convictions. For weeks, I found myself feeling vulnerable and anxious, my mind consumed with self-doubt, worry, and even a fear of judgment from others. It became clear that I needed to put a stop to this self-inflicted torture. I couldn't continue dragging myself through the abstinence hall of shame as if my life were over.

I made the decision to have a hard and honest chat with myself, acknowledging that I needed to seek counsel from someone who would not judge me or pry for unnecessary details. So, I reached out to a therapist whom I had spoken to before on other issues related to a career shift. I believed that having a thoughtful conversation with a trusted confidant would help me process my emotions and navigate the internal conflicts and personal concerns I was facing. Leading up to the encounter, I had communicated with my partner several times that I was on an abstinence journey, but I admit that my communication was not as assertive as it should have been. Additionally, I made the careless decision to place myself in an environment that did not support my goal, and I take full responsibility for that.

The most important lesson I have learned on my journey of abstinence is the importance of doing it for the right reasons. Abstinence should not be seen as a badge of honor used to boast about the number of years one has abstained, as that holds little significance for most individuals, especially men. Instead, it is crucial to embark on and maintain an abstinent lifestyle for the right motives. Personally, I have come to realize that my abstinence is deeply connected to my relationship with God and His desires for me as a human being. It aligns with what His word teaches about sexual purity. Once this understanding dawned on me, I no longer viewed my abstinence journey in terms of its duration. It has become a way of life, something I embrace because I am a child of the Divine, and it is what He expects from me.

I have since moved on from that person and that experience, and I no longer feel guilty about it. I recognize that as a human being I am prone to making mistakes, even in situations where my intentions are good. The most important thing I can do for myself now is to show myself compassion and forgiveness and to reflect on the lessons that can be learned from this experience.

Points to Ponder

- Identifying and defining your core values may seem overwhelming, but it is a worthwhile endeavour if you dedicate the necessary time to developing them.

- Remember that values can change over time as you have new experiences and evolve as a person. Your values are a good foundation for creating boundaries. Don't view your boundaries as invisible walls that you use to protect yourself from men, but rather a valuable tool for fostering respect and security. Without clearly stated boundaries, your suitor may not know what is acceptable or when he has crossed a line. With boundaries, codependency is less likely; boundaries allow each person in the relationship to maintain their own unique identity.

This chapter is an excerpt from my Amazon #1 new release titled *Delayed Not Denied: The Journey of Singleness—It's Worth the W.A.I.T.* The book is available in eBook and print on Amazon. Signed copies are available when purchased via my website. Use the QR code below.

Vanessa Ingrid Farrell

Vanessa Ingrid Farrell is a speaker, bestselling author, and CEO and founder of Vanessa Ingrid (VI) Health & Wellness Coaching, LLC. Her coaching practice helps busy women, especially those in leadership roles, unapologetically prioritize and preserve their heart health without sacrificing their careers and the joys of everyday life experiences.

Vanessa loves journaling and is a trained journal coach. She has been journaling for over 30 years and is a member of the International Association for Journal Writing. She facilitates individual and group journaling sessions and workshops, and she has created and published many journals.

Vanessa was born on the beautiful island of Montserrat in the Caribbean and currently resides on the island of St. Croix in the United States Virgin Islands. Vanessa is available virtually and in person for speaking engagements, workshops, and retreats.

Email: VFarrell@VIHealthcoaching.com

Website (and online journal store): www.vihealthcoaching.com

Chapter 10
Never Give Up—Growth Comes from Pushing

By The Tini Twins – Charlene & Chantelle Mahlatini

> *'Stay true to yourself, yet always be open to learn. Work hard, and never give up on your dreams, even when nobody else believes they can come true but you. These are not cliches but real tools you need no matter what you do in life to stay focused on your path.'*
>
> **– Phillip Sweet**

Many of us aspire to lead fulfilling lives, free from financial worries and enriched by exploration. The idea of creating our own business emerged as a pathway to realizing this vision—a journey toward a life of abundance and adventure. In pursuit of our dream life, we delved into the world of starting a fashion business. Through extensive research on Google and YouTube, we acquired the skills to build everything from the ground up. We scoured numerous websites in search of the perfect fabrics, mastered patternmaking, and honed our sewing abilities. A pivotal moment came with a pilgrimage to New York City, where we sourced materials from one of America's premier fabric stores. Armed with knowledge, we launched our Instagram account showcasing our designs, with swimwear emerging as our passion. In time, we began collaborating with women from neighboring cities, both as models and co-creators, fostering a brand ethos of empowerment and confidence, while honing their craft in front of the camera.

Despite facing financial constraints, our determination to produce high-quality swimsuits never wavered. While money posed a significant challenge, we remained undeterred, seeking additional employment opportunities to sustain our dream. Attending beauty school was a pivotal step in realizing our dream life. After graduating and obtaining licenses, we embarked on careers as stylists, laying the groundwork for the establishment of Glam by Tini Twins within two years. This venture has proven to be our most lucrative, providing the financial foundation to support the growth of Latini Couture, our first business endeavor. Though progress was gradual, perseverance prevailed, and over the course of a few years, we successfully brought our vision to life.

Our journey was profoundly shaped by the unwavering support of our mom, who served as a pillar of encouragement and motivation, enabling us to translate our plans into action. Additionally, our grandmother played a pivotal role in influencing our path toward the fashion world. Witnessing her entrepreneurial spirit firsthand as she sold knitted clothing and managed a convenience store left an indelible impression on us, igniting our desire to carve out our own path. Moreover, being surrounded by a family of entrepreneurs, including our aunts and uncles, instilled in us a deep-seated entrepreneurial drive that was ingrained in our upbringing.

In addition, working at our aunt's salon, Star Kreations, provided us with invaluable insights into the hair industry. This experience not only honed our skills but also deepened our understanding of customer service, trends, and the business aspects of running a successful salon. It was here that we truly grasped the importance of passion and precision in crafting one's skill, lessons that have been instrumental in our journey.

In pursuit of our dreams, we encountered numerous sacrifices, including taking on jobs that didn't align with our passions, to sustain our small business. Despite facing occasional lack of support from friends and family, we remained steadfast in our resolve to persevere. As we progressed, our priorities and values underwent a transformation, crystallizing around the belief that pursuing our passion was the key to living the abundant life we desired. Embracing the journey of fulfilling our own dreams became intertwined with our mission to inspire others to do the same. Creating a nurturing environment where women could authentically express themselves while chasing their aspirations became our driving force and source of fulfillment.

Indeed, this journey has been transformative, not just for us but for our entire family, marking the inception of a new generational milestone. Along the way, we encountered obstacles we never thought possible to overcome, yet through perseverance, we emerged stronger than ever. Our journey has served as a beacon of inspiration for both women and men, urging them to believe in themselves above all else. Through this experience, we've gained invaluable insights into the essence of entrepreneurship: patience, consistency, and unwavering dedication. We've learned that success doesn't happen overnight; it's a daily commitment to our dreams. Amidst the chaos of business ownership, it's crucial to stay grounded in our initial motivations, reminding ourselves why we embarked on this journey in the first place. Each day presents a new opportunity to pursue our dream life with clarity and purpose.

Our greatest achievement lies in the inspiration we've ignited in others to pursue their entrepreneurial dreams. One significant milestone we celebrated was selling over 1,000 masks during the challenging times of COVID-19. Looking ahead, we are thrilled about our upcoming milestone—our inaugural celebrity collaboration collection with the renowned singer and actress Jessica Jarrell.

Reflecting on our journey, the advice we would impart to our past selves is simple yet profound: Never give up. We would emphasize the importance of staying focused on doing what we love, even when faced with challenges. Growth often comes from pushing ourselves beyond our comfort zones and embracing tasks we may not initially enjoy. It's these experiences that pave the way for progress and lead us to the next level of success. Keep going!

With love,

The Tini Twins

The Tini Twins
– Charlene & Chantelle Mahlatini

Charlene and Chantelle Mahlatini are the dynamic, personable twin sister duo popularly known as the Tini Twins. Their passion for beauty and fashion led them to establish a successful beauty salon—Glam by Tini Twins—and a fashion line—Latini Couture—where they offer top-notch services to their clients. In addition to running their salon, they are actively involved in social media as content creators, sharing their expertise in cosmetology, fashion, inspiration, motivation, and encouragement with a wide audience. With a keen eye for style and a deep understanding of the latest trends in the beauty industry, the Tini Twins have built a strong online presence, attracting followers who look to them for inspiration and advice. Their dedication to their craft and their commitment to providing exceptional beauty services have earned them a reputation as respected figures in the beauty and fashion community.

Chapter 11
From Dreams to Reality
By Dr. Stem Sithembile Mahlatini

Dare to live the life you have dreamed for yourself. Go forward and make your dreams come true.

– Ralph Waldo Emerson

Dreams can be wishes for a better life, or they can be hopes for a fun adventure. If you are dreaming and talking about your dreams and desires, that usually means you want something more. It usually means you think there is something more you can do with your life. It doesn't have to mean your current life is bad or not enough; you should always find happiness where you are. There are, however, so many possibilities for a life of joy, health, wealth, and happiness that it would be foolish not to wish for more. You should never stop dreaming of new adventures. You are not here to survive but to thrive.

Believe in what you want so much that it has no choice but to materialize.

A Few of My Dreams

- Start a successful private practice for training, coaching, and counseling. (This came true—I own Global Training, Coaching and Consulting Services, Inc.)

- Start an online empowerment academy for women and youth. (This came true—I own The DrStem Empowerment Academy, where you can join the exciting, empowering MyBestLife Tribe membership for women aspiring to live healthier, happier, wealthier lifestyles.)

- Become an author. (This happened—I have authored and co-authored over 52 books.)

- Start the annual Bounce Back Empowerment Academy and the *Bounce Back* book series. (This happened—2024 is our fifth annual Bounce Back Empowerment Conference.)

- Start a collaboration with new and seasoned authors and publish Bounce back Anthology (Happening, so excited this 2024 we are releasing this Vol 2 Bounce Back Book)

- Conduct Bounce Back Empowerment Workshops and Seminars; Virtual and in Person (Coming Soon)

- Travel with the Bounce Back Conference around the United States and the world. (This is happening.)

- Speak around the world as a motivational speaker. (This is happening.)

- Host a TV/radio show. (This is happening. Check out the DrStem Show on YouTube and all podcast platforms.)

- Start a Non Profit For Women and Youth Empowerment Services, W-YES registered in Boston and Florida (starting Nov 2024)

Never Stop Dreaming Dreams Do Come True!

What Are Your Dreams?
Do Any of These Ideas Sound Familiar?

- Find a better-paying job
- Build a new house or buy a lake home
- Retire early or work from home
- Go to the Super Bowl
- Go on a safari
- Start your own business
- Lose weight or get healthy
- Star in a movie
- Become an author
- Start your own business
- Get a job promotion
- Go back to school

> *The future belongs to those who believe in the beauty of their dreams.*
>
> **—Eleanor Roosevelt**

Making your dreams come true is all up to you—you have to make those dreams come true. When I say this, many people look at me and say, "Yeah, right. Where do I even start?"

Here are some strategies that might help you with taking that first step:

1. Visualize Your Dreams

Get clear on what you want. Create a vision board. Cut out pictures that match what you want your dreams to look like and paste them on a poster board. Put your board somewhere you will see it every day. Take five minutes each day to visualize yourself fulfilling those dreams. See and feel yourself in those moments. Believe you can achieve them. Write your vision and desires down in your journal every day! Make it a mantra or affirmation and post it on your mirror or refrigerator. See yourself living your dreams—picture yourself in your new house, married to the love of your life, running a successful business, and more.

2. Tell Others About Your Dreams

Yes, be comfortable saying your dreams out loud. As you continually talk about your dreams, you believe in them more. It also holds you accountable to achieve them, and who knows, you might tell someone who can help make them happen! Find a friend with whom you can play make-believe. Tell each other all the wonderful things happening in your life as if they were true.

3. Take Steps to Plan Your Dreams

Do your research on what it would take to fulfill your dreams. Think through all of the details. Break these down into workable steps and set a timeframe. Hire a coach who can help you get clear on what you want and support you in taking actions that will make your dreams come true.

4. Be Happy Where You Are

When you are happy with your life, you are more productive, creative, energized, charismatic, and influential—all of which are great strengths to help you work out your plan. Don't wait for your dream to come true to be happy. Be happy now, and the energy to create will help you have an open mind and open heart to explore and receive new opportunities. Enjoy the journey and then bask in your achievement!

5. Start Now

There is no greater time than now to start living your dreams. But how do you do it? Making your dreams come true doesn't have to be a wild fantasy—you can begin achieving your dreams today! Every day is an opportunity to work towards your dreams and desires. You have to be intentional and make time for your dreams. Once you make time, make sure you use that time wisely—be productive.

6. Break Down the Steps You Need to Take for Your Dreams to Become a Reality

Think about what you want to achieve in detail and then picture yourself accomplishing that goal. Break down your dreams into small, measurable steps, and take action to achieve them. Believe in yourself, don't be discouraged by setbacks, and give yourself time to relax and recharge.

7. Be Specific About Your Dreams

Think of it this way: If you don't know what you really want, how can you achieve it? As I mentioned before, write your dreams down in a notebook or on your phone as if they were attainable goals. What do you need to accomplish them? How can you make progress each day? For example, let's say you want to be an accomplished writer. Take the time to think about what type of writer you want to be and ask yourself what you really want? If you want to write a book, then that might involve writing a chapter each day. Don't worry if you don't have it all figured out—just be as specific as possible.

8. Turn Your Dreams into Desires

A strong will to achieve your dreams boosts self-confidence and helps motivate you. Have full belief in your dreams— you *can* and *will* achieve them. Look at your dreams as things that fuel you rather than tasks that have to get done. I am a member of an online platform, named Kajabi, where there are also hundreds of thousands of multi-millionaires. I am encouraged, inspired, and empowered every day to elevate my game and pursue my dreams because I have seen many of these individuals start from scratch just like I did, and now they are multi-millionaires. It's possible— *dreams do come true*; this I know and believe.

9. Make Time to Review Your Progress Regularly

As you start on the path to making your dreams come true, it's important to have a sense of what you are accomplishing. Even if you're not moving as quickly as you'd like, you're still moving forward and making progress. Here are some questions that have helped me out as I developed my personal progress report:

- Have I achieved my goals for that time period?
- Do I still have a desire to follow this dream? What am I doing to continue motivating myself?
- Have I deviated from the path towards fulfilling my goal? If yes, how can I get back on track?
- Am I having fun and enjoying my journey? If the answer is no, ask yourself, "What can I do to make sure I am having fun and enjoying working towards achieving my dreams?"

10. Stay Motivated by Continuing to Visualize Your Success

Close your eyes and picture what your life will be like when your dream comes true. Imagine the excitement and joy you'll experience when your dream does become a reality. This can help you feel motivated when you're stuck or feeling down.

11. Make Time to Relax—Self-Care Is Critical

While it's important to be persistent about following your dreams and achieving your goals, it's just as equally important to take some time off to rest. Avoid burnout and stress by getting enough sleep each night and doing other things you enjoy. The time away from your goals or dreams can actually make you more eager to accomplish them. Relax your mind with exercise, meditation, or yoga. Get frequent massages and acupuncture. Aim to get at least seven hours of sleep each night.

12. Believe in Yourself—Believe You Can

Believe it is possible for you. Being confident and self-assured is a great way to stay on track. When you believe in yourself, it can be easier to keep moving forward, even when things get tough. If you believe you can do it, there's nothing that can stop you. Say positive things to yourself throughout the day. A quick, encouraging affirmation like, "I can do this" or "I am capable," can help lift your spirits.

13. Learn from Failures and Mistakes

If you want to achieve your dreams, then you have to be able to learn from setbacks. Mistakes give you an opportunity to grow and evolve. If you've failed at something, ask yourself why it happened and what you could have done differently. Then, use this knowledge as you continue chasing your dreams. Instead of letting setbacks bring you down, use them to get more eager to achieve your goal.

14. Accept Constructive Criticism Along the Way

This is key. I have learned I do not know everything. I need help, new information, and guidance every so often. I have also learned that although it's important to stay focused on your goal, listening to the people trying to help you is just as important. While you don't have to listen to every critic, keep an open mind. Many people mean well. Who knows—you may just learn something new that will get you living your dream quicker than you know. Remember, though, use your best judgment when handling criticism, as not everyone has your best interest in mind.

15. *Make the Necessary Sacrifices You Need to Make*

You may have to give up some things to make your dreams happen. You may have to stay in to study instead of hanging out with friends, you may have to say no to an unrelated opportunity in order to have more time to follow your dreams, or perhaps you may have to stay longer in a position while you work towards your dreams. Sacrifices aren't easy, but sometimes they're necessary and rewarding in the end.

16. *Set Clear Boundaries for Yourself and Loved Ones*

Why? You set clear boundaries with yourself and loved ones so you can stay on track with your plan. For instance, you might give yourself a strict bedtime so you can wake up early and train for a marathon, write that book, study for that program, or record your digital course.

Bonus 1. Remove Any Obstacles Standing in Your Way

Think about it: What is keeping you from achieving your goals right now? What's holding you back? If something or someone is preventing you from allowing your dreams to come true, consider what you have to do to remove the problem. For example, maybe you have a toxic friend who gets hostile when you can't hang out with them. Perhaps it's time to pause the friendship and give yourself some space.

As another example—say you have a habit of watching TV before bed, but now you want to read 100 books this year. Removing the TV from your bedroom may help you accomplish your goal faster. I did this, and it has helped me tremendously. My bedroom is for rest, and I use what once was "TV time" more wisely and productively.

Bonus 2. Drop the Excuses

Life happens, and things can go awry, but that doesn't mean you should stop reaching for the stars! You don't always have to put your dreams on hold. Avoid making excuses for why you haven't accomplished your daily tasks or progressed any further with your plan. Rather than saying, "I can't," try saying, "I will." What dreams are you ready to make come true? Start writing in your journal today. Here is to every one of your dreams coming true—they will.

All our dreams can come true if we have the courage to pursue them.

– *Walt Disney*

If you want a thing bad enough to go out and fight for it, to work day and night for it, and to give up your time, your peace, and your sleep for it; If all that you dream and scheme is about it, and life seems useless and worthless without it; If you gladly sweat for it, fret for it, plan for it, and lose all your terror of the opposition for it; If you simply go after that thing that you want with all your capacity, strength, sagacity, faith, hope, confidence, and stern pertinacity; If neither cold, poverty, famine, nor gout, sickness, or pain of body and brain can keep you away from the thing that you want; If dogged and grim you besiege and beset it—with the help of God, *you will get it*!

As I end this chapter, I have a special invitation for you or anyone you know. If you have ever thought of writing a book, or you are a published author looking to expand your reach, I would like to invite you to be a co-author with us. We welcome you to the *Bounce Back* author family. Email me at drstem14@gmail.com for more information or connect with me at www.drstemmie.com.

Be encouraged!
Dr. Stem Sithembile Mahlatini

Originally from Zimbabwe, **Dr. Stem Sithembile Mahlatini** is a confidence coach, resident, and owner of Global Counseling and Coaching Services, Inc. and founder of The Empowerment Academy, an online platform with life success programs, workshops, seminars, and books. Her mission is to inspire, empower, and educate others to live stress-free, successful lives through her speaking engagements, books, seminars, workshops, counseling, and coaching services. In addition, she hosts The Dr. Stem Show Radio, Television, and Podcast, which is an educational, empowerment, and encouragement show. You can find her shows on YouTube and all podcast platforms.

Drawing on her background as a licensed psychotherapist, Dr. Stem offers people practical advice on how to tap into their limitless power to change their lives, overcome roadblocks, and aspire to be better than the circumstances that surround them. For businesses, she provides cutting-edge training and coaching programs to help business leaders and employees break through personal and environmental barriers to maximize their success in all areas of their lives. Her lifelong goal is to continue to help others build unshakable confidence to be winners at home, work, and business. Her motto is: "Each day is an opportunity to become more confident, successful, and happy."

Websites: www.drstemmie.com
www.drstemspeaks.com
www.womenyouthservices.com

Chapter 12
Me, Life, and God

By Vanessa Maldonado

Don't ever let someone tell you that you can't do something. You got a dream, you gotta protect it. When people can't do something themselves, they are going to tell you that you can't do it. You want something, go get it. Period. Will Smith

– Pursuit of Happyness

Life contains an abundance of emotions, changes, and growth. I can tell you my life is far from perfect, as perfection is not a standard anyone can live up to. However, I know it is a blessing from God that I have had the chance to wake up every day and be grateful for the life I live. As I begin to tell my story, I want to ask everyone to tap into your hearts and think back in your life to your years as a teenager and in your early 20s. What did you accomplish? Have you felt heartbreak? Were there any new additions in your life? Did you pray and ask God why certain things were occurring during this time? These are key questions I have asked myself many, many, many times. The wonderful part about what I have realized from the answers to these questions is that they were all part of God's plan.

As a little girl, I never would have imagined I would go through so many phases in such a short time in life—from being homeless with my family for a couple of months, to graduating high school with such a low GPA I could barely apply to the universities I truly wanted, to a bundle of joy my freshmen year in college, to losing one of the most important men in my life when my college experience was coming to an end. There are so many things we go through as humans that we cannot be prepared for, but with God, He is just, He heals all, and He has reconstructed my heart.

It all started in the hospital on September 18, 1995, in Bridgeport, Connecticut. I was born at around six pounds at about 5 a.m. on a Monday. My mother was filled with joy, as she did not only have one little bun in the oven but two. Following me entering the world came my twin sister; however, she was not ready and began moving backwards, climbing up and gripping on to my mother's lungs. After many hours and a restless night for my mother, my sister safely entered the world through a c-section.

Growing up, my mother was determined to give us a life without worries. There were four of us—my older brother, older sister, me, and my twin. When my twin sister and I were about the age of 4, and my other siblings a bit older than that, my mother made the move to Salem, Massachusetts after separating from my father. Through our rough years growing up, where my mom worked endlessly to ensure we had food on the table, we would all play, fight, and bicker, but our sibling love was unbreakable. We had a very blessed life because that is what we made it. Our mother worked hard and made sure to raise her kids in a happy home, no matter what the circumstances were. She was so strong, fierce, and loving. She loved her children and would fight till the end of the world for us. She truly is our roots to our hearts. No matter what, a mother's love is stronger than anyone in the world—she will protect, she will provide, and she will sacrifice.

Let's fast forward in life a little bit. During my middle school years, I began to grow as a young girl. My body was changing, and I began to make outfit decisions and interesting hair choices. I got my first cellphone when I was in eighth grade, and I remember being so sad when I got it taken away for a weekend after misbehaving in school. I had some anger issues that I needed to get under control during that time. I began talking back to my mom—I don't know if it was the pressure of schoolwork or going through my menstrual cycle or both.

My twin and I shared a room. We would have nights of laughter and sometimes nights of bickering about cleanliness. I was very particular with my clothes and placement of items. My twin? Well, she was not. My mother ensured we lived a clean lifestyle, though, and chores were completed on a weekly basis—early Saturday morning with fun Hispanic music.

Once eighth grade graduation had occurred, it meant stepping into a new era in my life—high school—where I found new friends and interests. High school was an entirely different experience for me, one that did not seem like anything I could have imagined, from not taking grades seriously to losing a friend during my first year. This was a friend who I had gone through elementary school with. I received a phone call on a Friday night saying he had taken his own life—he had committed suicide. I stopped and thought to myself, "Why, why take your precious life away? Why did you make the decision to stop your own journey?" It did not make sense to me; however, I was one who also faced challenges with my own spirit. I, too, was part of a cycle. I dealt with depression, anxiety, and not ever feeling like enough. I had thoughts cross my mind and would ask myself, "Will everyone's life be better without me in it?" But then I knew—it was not my thought but that of the enemy, trying to push and pull me into a force that was dark and unwavering. I could not fall into this trap. I could not give in.

That same year, my freshman year, I met Dr. Stem Malatini. She is one of the many reasons why I have the light I carry today. Dr. Stem is one of the many blessings I have encountered in my life. She is a gift from God in my life. She has helped me overcome and change as a young woman. She has helped me not only spiritually but emotionally. I have an endless love for her and the words she has shared with me in our past conversations. I will never forget the day she informed me of the battles I face within myself—she diagnosed me with depression and anxiety. I told her that I refused to take medication, and I would not commit to allowing the American culture to convince me of needing a drug in order for the chemicals inside my body to align. I looked up at her and said, "There is a God, and there is a way—He will not fail me." From then on, I have always had faith in God to help me on my journey.

When I graduated high school in 2014, I had no idea what I wanted to do or who I wanted to become. All I knew was that I had to go to college—I needed to obtain a four-year degree in something. However, as I was beginning this new stage of my journey, a surprise came along quick—I found out I was pregnant in

November of that same year. I had a healthy pregnancy and was blessed to give birth to my beautiful baby girl, Audrey, on July 21, 2015. I was still living at home with my mom as I took some time off of work and school. However, I battled with post-partum depression, lost weight, and started losing myself. I felt I did not know how to think, act, or even breathe. My body changed after giving birth, almost as if it was trying to readjust itself back to normal. Barely sleeping, unable to thrive as a mother since I was still learning to be a young adult myself, I felt my life was collapsing. I knew I had to get busy and find work. I started working just two months after giving birth. I managed being a waitress for a short period of time and then switched professions over the years.

I took a semester off from school to figure out life and settle in with my daughter. I returned in the spring of 2016, with a welcome back from the trio team. I knew I needed to start figuring out the classes I was going to take and begin exploring my major. I had options, and it was overwhelming. I thought about education, criminal justice, business management, and psychology. I took some classes within each of these subjects and withdrew from a lot of them. I could not keep up with the schoolwork because of the many things happening in my life outside of being a part-time student. It was as if I could not catch a break—I felt I was drowning being a mother, going to school, and working to be financially stable for my family.

As you know, life does not stop for anyone—it keeps on going, regardless of how challenging it becomes. Time is the most valuable thing we have on this Earth because life is short. We never know when the day will come where someone we love dearly will be gone. In the year 2019, I began to feel as though things were falling into place in my life. I was growing in my career at the time, and my daughter was growing into a beautiful, independent, strong, little girl. My older sister had just gotten married to the love of her life in August of 2018, and my father was able to walk her down the aisle.

It was on January 12, 2019, that my life changed. I had lost half of myself…. It was announced that my father, Edwin Maldonado, had been pronounced dead in his home. My grandfather found him leaning over in the bathroom with the door locked. I was getting ready for work that morning, thinking it was another blessed day to be alive. My mother rushed down the stairs and screamed my name as she ran to me, informing me my father was dead; she hugged me and started crying. I pulled away and told her that it was not true… it could not be true. My mother held me and cried on my shoulder. In that very moment, I felt my soul had left my body, my heart had been ripped out of my chest. I was in disbelief. My daughter was 3 years old and not able to grasp the situation. I knew I needed to gather myself, so my family and I could rush to Waterbury, Connecticut.

A death in anyone's life can change you as a person. I was angry; I questioned my faith in God and how this would pull me closer to Him. The truth is that I distanced myself from God. I did not know how to go on with my life when someone so important had left me. The truth is my father was suffering, and he had been for a long time. He was diabetic and had dealt with three open-heart surgeries. His health was his lifeline, and I missed all the signs. It took about a year and a half for me to heal and let go of my anger. With God hearing me and giving His grace, I was able to continue to live and find happiness with the life He had created for me.

In 2020, I was finishing college; however, this was also the year that the world was dealing with the devastating news of COVID-19 — a new disease, a new virus, a new silent killer. I had to move from in-person classes to finishing the year virtually. With all these life changes, I had to come to terms with not having a traditional graduation ceremony. It was not celebrated in any of the ways you can imagine, so I decided to not attend and celebrated with my friends and family instead. I attended Salem State University for a total of almost six years, and I finished having to settle for a limited ceremony.

Within the year, I went from a relationship with a man who I thought I was going to marry to a new career as a social worker for the state. In that same year, though, I started to lose sight of who I was. I had so much anger within me—a lot of this stemming from what people thought of me and of how I was as a daughter, sister, and mother. I had a lot of pressure trying to be this perfect person in the eyes of others. However, I could not be perfect. There was no such thing as perfection. I needed to let go; I needed to seek something more.

My best friend, Jay, introduced me to Eagle Heights Cathedral, a church that I entered and felt warmth but lost at the same time. The lost feeling was not the church—it was an emptiness within me. When I grew up, church was never so vibrant and full of life. I remember being a miserable little girl forced to go to Sunday service. This place was different. Bishop Collins opened my heart to the words God would lead him to share with the church. I had never felt so much joy walking into a service and feeling like I was meant to be there. My journey began here. It's been a rocky path, but God is still working with me and my heart.

We live in a time where people feel free to express themselves—whether we agree with them or not, they live a free life. God has given us the choice to live a life of free will, and it is what we choose that can affect our current life situations. I gave my life to God on April 7, 2023, and was baptized by Bishop Collins and the church Eagle Heights Cathedral. I chose this path to live a righteous life. It took time, healing, understanding, trials, and losses for me to get to where I am, and there is still so much work that needs to be done. It was not easy; my spirit was shifted and tested on a daily basis. There were many times I felt I kept getting pushed away and then pulled into continuing bad habitats from my past, whether it was with my family or fights starting with my best friend. I just did not know why certain things were happening. I felt so torn and alone. Once I let go, though, I was reborn. This was it—I needed to lean on God. I needed to turn away from the forces that were trying to pull at me. I prayed, I began to read the Bible, and I started going to church more. I began to feel fulfilled in ways I cannot explain. God is real, and He will provide. He is just!

I can write of the trials and tribulations I have faced, but it is this message that I leave you with: It is just the beginning to more blessings and a better life. If I could give my younger self any advice, I would say: "Pray and leave it in His hands. Trust in Him, and you will live a fruitful life. There will be days that are gray and days that are darker than others, but the light always shines, even in those darkest days. Don't lose sight, and most importantly, do not lose faith."

Vanessa Maldonado

Vanessa Maldonado, BA, a proud mother to her 8-year-old daughter, Audrey Blair Demoya, was born in Bridgeport, Connecticut, on September 18, 1995. At the age of 4, she moved to Salem, Massachusetts, where she attended Salem Public Schools. During her high school years, she met Dr. Stem, who had a profound impact on her life and helped shape her into the woman she is today. Vanessa graduated from Salem High School in 2014 and continued her education at Salem State University, where she graduated with a degree in sociology and a minor in English. She currently works at Salem High School.

Chapter 13

The Meaning of Faith Over Fear to Me

By Nicole Marange

"Are you facing fear today? Perhaps you are afraid of losing your job, of developing cancer, or being left by your spouse. At times all of us experience fear. But don't allow fear to keep you from being used by God. He has kept you thus far; trust Him for the rest of the way."

– Woodrow Kroll

I have never written a book before, I have decided to write my chapter in a question and answer format. I hope this will resonate with someone and help you as you journey through life with faith and not fear.

What does faith mean to you personally? How would you define faith in the context of overcoming fear and challenges?

Faith, for me, is something that is personal and all mine. It is something I can always rely on when everything seems uncertain. When I am fearful, my faith gives me the strength to believe that there is a bigger plan out there for me. I view faith as an inner voice that gives me the best pep talks. I can hear it now as l write this, whispering, "Keep going, you've got this," and that voice gives me the strength to get through challenges.

Can you recall a specific moment in your life when you had to choose between succumbing to fear or relying on faith? How did you navigate this situation?

Recently, I decided to move back home. I was very afraid of what lies ahead for my future, but l decided to rely on faith and make the move. The way l decided to navigate this transition was to constantly pray and rely on my family and friends to help and comfort me. In the end, I knew I needed to just give the situation to God. Luckily, this has all worked out. l still have some things to figure out but, so far, as long as l rely on my faith to guide me, it has not steered me wrong.

How do you cultivate and strengthen your faith in times of uncertainty or difficulty? Are there specific practices or beliefs that help you maintain your faith?

Sometimes it can feel as though walls are caving in, and uncertainty is all that surrounds me. This, for me, is the best time to use prayer. Prayer has always had my back, and it is something that always reassures me. I can engage in it anywhere, and l can present all of my concerns to God. I don't have to be ashamed because l can relax and know that God is listening and taking care of all my worries. There is a comfort in knowing this truth like no other.

One of my favourite things to do is watch movies about Bible stories. This really gives me a new level of understanding that I believe some people in today's world need in order for them to grasp the reality of the stories that are told in the Bible. Another thing I enjoy doing is surrounding myself with those who share a similar faith because this allows for me to constantly learn new things and share my faith with others. Specific practices that help me maintain my faith are prayer, attending church, and being surrounded by my family. These are my biggest support systems, and they always remind me to turn to my faith when in doubt.

What role does fear play in your life, and how does it impact your decision-making and actions? How do you work to overcome fear when faced with challenges?

Fear is like hunger; eventually it creeps up in my life no matter what I do, and it certainly plays a larger role in my life than I would like. Overcoming fear is something that requires constant effort. There are a lot of things that make me fearful, and oftentimes this impacts my ability to make decisions. Fear can make me say no when I want to say yes. It can also make me less confident in my decisions, forcing me to reconsider decisions I've already made, and even influence me enough to make a different decision than I would have originally made if it wasn't for fear.

I work to overcome my fear by getting as many no's as possible. I also try to seek out rejection sometimes because it helps keep the fear at bay. Another thing I like to do is communicate my fears to my family and peers and seek advice from them. Hearing an outside perspective can make my fears seem like they're not so bad. Lastly, I like to apply the three-second rule, which means, within three seconds, I have to do the thing that makes me fearful. This exercise forces me to stop thinking and just take a step forward.

Can you share a story or anecdote that illustrates a time when your faith helped you overcome a significant obstacle or fear?

When I was younger and trying to make a cheer competition team, I had to learn how to do a backflip. I was terrified because I had heard so many horror stories of people breaking their neck, back, arms, legs, or even becoming paralyzed if the backflip went wrong. In order to join the competition team, however, I was required to learn this skill. I prayed every night about doing this backflip, and I decided to let go of my fears and give this situation over to God. I truly felt His spirit and trusted the people who were monitoring me. When the time came to perform the backflip, I went for it and landed it on the first try. To me, this was a true testament of faith over fear. After this experience, I was no longer afraid to do the flip, I continued to get better at the skill, and I was able to join the team. In the end, I prayed and thanked God that I was safe and healthy and a part of the competition team. It was my first taste of how powerful faith can be if you truly believe.

How do you differentiate between rational caution and paralyzing fear? How does faith guide you in making decisions in challenging situations?

Rational caution is a measured response based on real risks. It considers the situation, weighs potential dangers, and prompts you to take appropriate precautions. Fear, however, is an overwhelming emotional reaction that can distort reality. It makes small dangers out to be monstrous or good opportunities seem like they are destined to end in doom. Faith, in this context, isn't about blind trust, but it is about the core beliefs that provide strength and direction. Faith helps me navigate challenges by reminding me of my values. This gives me a sense of calm when l am feeling unsure and motivates me to take smart risks that are morally sound to me.

In what ways does faith empower you to take risks and step outside of your comfort zone? How has this mindset contributed to your personal growth and resilience?

Faith gives me a sense of purpose and security. Believing in God allows me to not fear failure and the unknown. Faith actually gives me a feeling that even if something goes wrong, there is a bigger plan at work. It also teaches me to have courage and compassion. When there is a decision to be made, and it is a risky one, my faith can help me make the decision and remind me of my values and my morals. Those around me who share the same faith have become a community of support, and this has largely contributed to my personal growth and resilience. Stepping out of my comfort zone gives me the ability to try new things, build confidence, and achieve amazing feats.

How do you support others in cultivating faith and overcoming fear? What advice or guidance would you offer to someone who is struggling with fear and uncertainty?

One of the ways I support cultivating someone else's faith is by sharing information that l know. If someone lacks knowledge or understanding about other religions, I may be able to present what I have learned about these religions to this person. That, in turn, could help them decide what religion suits them best.

One of the things I love doing is sharing stories and practices that involve my faith. This often inspires others and teaches them something new they can learn from or follow. I may also be able to support others by acting as a guide for individuals who are trying to figure out their core values. When I feel that fear is holding someone back, I can help them connect their fear to their values and figure out how taking a risk may actually go along with their beliefs and values.

The guidance I would give someone is providing positive reinforcement as they navigate the challenges they are currently facing. Encouragement can help build their confidence and motivate them to continue pushing through the difficult time. What I would tell someone who is struggling with fear and uncertainty is to acknowledge the fear rather than try to ignore it, which likely will only make it worse.

I would also recommend starting to overcome your challenges with small steps and building from there. If you can, breaking down the challenge helps with confidence and allows for the bigger challenges to seem less daunting. I would encourage someone to focus on the present and stay in the moment. This will help with one's anxiety around the situation. Lastly, I would reassure the idea that everyone gets scared at some point, and this is normal. Even the most successful people have been scared— don't let fear hold you back from achieving your goals.

How does the concept of faith intersect with other values such as courage, perseverance, and hope? How do these values work together to help you navigate life and challenges?

Faith is a powerful fuel for courage, perseverance, and hope. It can be a foundation that gives you reason. Faith also helps to cultivate courage and risk-taking in order to step out of your comfort zone. It can give you a feeling of stability and a reason to get through difficult times. When you are faced with obstacles, faith helps give you the strength to persevere. It can help remind you that this is a temporary obstacle, and once overcome, the potential for a period of smooth sailing is on the horizon. Lastly, faith can give you hope for a positive outcome. It gives you the ability to believe that things will get better.

These values can be compared to the inner workings of a car—courage is the gas, perseverance is the engine, and hope is the battery. All of these things, when used together, help me navigate life and its challenges. I am able to tap into what I need in the moment to help me. For example, if I undergo major surgery to fix a persistent issue, it would be my faith that I would rely on to strengthen my spirits. This faith would fuel my courage to undergo the surgery and ignite my perseverance to endure the challenges, see the journey as worthwhile, and give me hope for a full recovery.

Looking ahead, how do you envision continuing to prioritize faith over fear in your future endeavours and experiences? What goals or aspirations do you hope to achieve through this mindset?

I envision continuing to prioritize my faith over fear in my future endeavours by expanding my knowledge of both my faith and the faith of others. This allows me to better understand the power of faith that other people are experiencing as well. Gaining greater insight from others also allows for the potential of helping me eliminate my own biases and becoming better at responding with a mindset of hope for a positive outcome. This will help counteract the negative and fear-based thinking I naturally possess. With my faith, my goal is to be a resource that fosters understanding, reduces fear, and encourages people to embrace the challenges of life with courage and hope.

Nicole Marange

Nicole Marange is a dynamic media marketing expert known for her enthusiasm, vivacious personality, and go-getter attitude. As a role model and older sister to her two siblings, Martin and Michael, she embodies dedication and perseverance in all her endeavors.

With a passion for media and marketing, Nicole aspires to establish her own business in the field. Her creative vision, strategic thinking, and strong leadership skills set her apart in the competitive world of media marketing. Known for her innovative ideas and ability to adapt to changing trends, Nicole is a trailblazer in the industry.

Nicole's strong work ethic and commitment to excellence make her a valuable asset to any team. Her positive attitude and natural charisma inspire those around her to reach their full potential. With a deep understanding of media platforms and consumer behavior, Nicole is poised to make a significant impact in the world of marketing.

In her free time, Nicole enjoys spending quality time with her siblings, exploring new opportunities for growth and learning, and giving back to her community. With her unwavering determination and drive for success, Nicole Marange is a rising star in the world of media marketing, destined to achieve great things in her career.

Chapter 14

From Fear to Reality: Finances

By Gary Moses

> *"I say, choose faith. Choose faith over doubt, choose faith over fear, choose faith over the unknown and the unseen, and choose faith over pessimism."*
>
> *– Dallin H. Oaks*

Fear of a bank... fear of credit... fear of saving... fear of a mortgage... fear of generational wealth... do these concerns resonate with you? Do you want generational wealth but do not trust financial institutions and bankers out of fear they might not have your best interest in mind? Let's start with the end goal—to create wealth and pass it down, allowing it to grow over generations. Does this sound familiar? For most of us, finances are a four-letter word—we smile and nod our heads but don't want to broach the subject for fear of embarrassment. Why be embarrassed, though? Are we expected to know? Of course not, so stop acting like you are supposed to understand. What we are supposed to know is how to take charge of finances, not have finances take charge of us. How do we do this?

Education

This doesn't have to be formal education in the form of college or beyond; education can be gained from a myriad of sources such as books, online, subject matter experts (SME's), and even television. The key is to open your mind to being exposed to a different thought process, so the fear isn't passed down instead of the wealth. In the United States, over 85% of Americans do not have a savings account, and that number is higher amongst low- to moderate-income individuals (LMI). Why is this? Many LMI individuals do not understand the concept of a relationship with a bank or a banker. This may be because they have had one or more negative experiences and have since ruled traditional financial institutions out, favoring cash advance or check cashing locations instead.

Have you ever heard, "The bank took my money... they charge too many fees... how can I afford to save when you charge for everything?" Think about this concept: You pay a check cashing company to cash your check instead of depositing that same check into your own bank account at no fee, thereby having access to all your hard-earned money. One might say, "There will be a hold, and I need my money." Okay, sign up for direct deposit from your employer; the money is typically there by the time you wake up in the morning. Another response may be, "I don't have access to direct deposit." Okay, establish a relationship with the same bank as your employer, and checks will not be held. If that is not an option, start your own relationship, and after 30 days, your checks typically won't be held anymore. Excuses live rent free in your head. It's time to kick them out by educating yourself and moving from fear to reality.

Credit

How many of you have heard, "I was always told to pay cash for everything"? That was fine in the 1950s, when credit wasn't a thing; however, we are in the 21st century and quickly moving toward a cashless society. It is time for you to drop that old myth and take a leap into 2024. Think about this: Have you attempted to purchase a car with no credit? It can be done, but you won't get close to the best financing, and most likely, it will come from a secondary financing source (high risk—high interest rates). Guess what? You are happy because you have a car that you are paying way too much for. The good thing about this transaction is that if it is a reputable financial institution, rather than a "buy here, pay here" place, they are reporting your activity to the credit bureaus. Hopefully this activity is all positive, but you control that. What about purchasing a home? Again, it can be done but at what cost? The higher the interest rates, the more of a downpayment that is necessary (which is forcing many people out of the game, or the American dream).

Credit is not a toy or a game—it is a useful tool that can be your best friend or your worst enemy. If you pay with a credit card, make sure to pay the balance back early, on time, or all at once. How does one do this? It is recommended you do not borrow more than you can realistically afford to pay back. What do you mean? Think of every purchase as a want or a need. For example—food is a need; jewelry is a want. Once you have established these inner boundaries, and your credit score is going up, then you can look at more wants from time to time. Credit scores range from 350-850—both of which can be achieved—the former by not paying your bills and being overextended and the latter by living within your means and paying your bills on time or early, thereby moving from fear to reality.

Saving

Again, 85% of Americans do not have a savings account or an emergency fund (six months' worth of living expenses). You can call it whatever you want—just pay yourself first. It is a very easy thing to do when you break it down in elementary terms. For example, what can you purchase with $10 that you can't purchase with $9? That extra dollar can go into your savings account. Sign up for your company's retirement plan (401k/403b) and take full advantage of the company match. After a few direct deposit checks, you won't miss the money that is amassing in your retirement account.

Go a step further and start a savings account at your local bank. Deposit your weekly Starbucks or Coke Zero money, and you will be amazed at how quickly it grows. There are many vehicles that can assist you with saving your money, but you must be disciplined. It is too easy to dip into it because it is there, but guess what? When the emergency comes, and the emergency fund is empty, what will you do? Saving is no longer a luxury. It should be practiced by everyone, from a very early age to adulthood. Evict the excuse, thereby moving from fear to reality.

Mortgage

There are few in this world who would rather rent instead of owning their own house. Fear stops many people from taking the initial step, and thus, missing out on building wealth. A house is the most significant purchase most people will ever have, and it comes with many benefits. From the simple—laying your head down under your own roof where you don't have to listen to neighbors through the walls—to building equity and thereby increasing your personal financial position and finally being part of a thriving community where you take pride in your investment. Do you think you would rather pay rent because owning a house is too expensive? Have you looked at rentals lately? If you are renting, you are already paying a mortgage—it is just someone else's. Long gone are the days of affordable rental units unless it is in a declining part of town, but even there they can be high. A house is not only your most significant purchase, but it is typically your largest asset and your largest transference of wealth to your surviving family after you die. Start small, purchase what you can afford, use your rental payments as a gauge of how much you can afford, and move from fear to reality.

Generational Wealth

What is this? Think of names like Rockefeller, Vanderbilt, Du Pont, and Carnegie. Notice I did not say Oprah Winfrey, Ervin "Magic" Johnson, or even Bill Gates. That is because the original four tasked their families with not losing the fortunes that they amassed, and the latter are just rich; they are not wealthy for this thought process, but rather, they have and are earning, and nothing has passed down to the next generation yet. To amass wealth, you must take risks—buy a home, save money, or start a business that is disruptive in the marketplace. Too many people live for today without regard for their lives tomorrow.

Many people say, "Why should I worry about the next generation? I live for today, in the moment, and spend everything that I earn." This is fine, but by doing this, your legacy is to start over, and by leaving nothing, there is no platform to start on. The next generation will have to start from the bottom, and in many cases, below the bottom, if you can imagine that. Wealth starts in two places—real estate and business—and owning property has always been a good gauge and source of wealth.

People purchase real estate as an investment, and before they know it, they have multiple properties that are producing income. There are corporate properties where individuals own the land, and these individuals are earning significant amounts of money due to long-term leases. For example, just because a CVS sits on the corner does not mean they own the land beneath the building or the building, for that matter. Can you imagine a 30-year lease from a Fortune 500 company, where you never worry about them paying you? To be in the right situation for this, you must have a vision. That means you might own a piece of land for some time before you are presented with an income-producing opportunity or an opportunity to sell. When the time arrives, you must be smart and intentional about what you want to gain from the transaction.

Not everyone is going to be Bill Gates or Nelson Rockefeller when starting a business, but when you can call it your own and put your full energy and focus into it, you typically give more to gain more. One location becomes two, and two become three, and three might become a franchise. You might have an idea for an application that takes off on the Internet, and suddenly you are a self-made millionaire, or better yet—a billionaire. Necessity is the mother of invention; that is why so many people so long-ago amassed fortunes. They saw the need for something and provided a solution, whether it was through shipping or the railroads. These things were necessary, and it was the ideas that spawned the wealth. Believe in yourself and remove the fear on your journey to reality. When you second guess yourself, you are releasing that unwanted tenant that is living rent-free in the back of your mind. Evict them once and for all.

Gary Moses

Gary Moses has been in the banking industry, including finance and accounting, for the greater part of 25 years. Immediate past positions include financial center manager with SunTrust Bank; market manager for Workplace Banking with PNC Bank, covering the Alabama, Florida Panhandle, and Middle Georgia market; and regional manager with RBC Bank, covering multiple regions in the state of Florida. For the past five years, Gary has been the banking center manager at the Winter Park office of First Horizon Bank.

Gary attended college at Hofstra University on Long Island, NY, where he and his wife of 34 years met. Gary also earned his MBA from Crummer Graduate School of Business at Rollins College in Winter Park. His primary focus includes business acquisition and building relationships, along with financial education within the community. He and his wife, Jean Ann, have two children, Danielle and Robert (Shanice), a grandson, Rakhi, and granddaughter, Zora. They can't forget to mention Peanut, their Chihuahua, and Brooklyn, their black Golden Doodle.

Over the years, being involved within the community has always been a top priority to assist in giving back. Some of Gary's involvements include: National Black MBA Association of Central Florida, VP of finance board member; Rollins College—Hamilton Holt School for Professional Advancement, board member; Pride Chamber, board member; and Our Lessons Learned, board member. Gary's past affiliations include: Florida Hospital Cancer Institute, board member (finance committee representing the cancer institute); UCF Technology Incubator—Seminole County, board member; East Orlando Area Chamber of Commerce, board member and treasurer; Disney NEC, advisory board member and participant; University of Central Florida McKnight Achievers, president of Seminole County Chapter; and Kids4Kids, board member.

Chapter 15

Unwavering Faith Amid The Storms

By Reverend Ever Vennah Mudambanuki

"Turn it right over to God and ask Him to solve it with you. Fear is keeping things in your own hands; faith is turning them over into the hands of God."

– E. Stanley Jones

Faith is not an emotion. It is a decision to stand on God's Word. I could not believe my eyes, and my ears could not accept the news, when my late son said, "Mom, I am in terrible pain; I cannot sleep." I got off my bed and sat close to him as he started crying louder, "Mommy, I am in pain." I wondered where the pain was coming from because we had had a good supper, evening prayer, and a little chat before we went to bed. Of course, I had spent that Friday of November 20th in downtown Mutare, shopping and planning for our trip to the United States. A miracle had happened—the two of us, mother and son, now had tickets to fly to America. His father was waiting for us to reunite and have our first Christmas in America.

The thoughts, preparations, and anticipations of coming to the United States were a big dream in themselves. As a young lady in my late 20s, I dreamt so passionately to study abroad. I remember applying to these big universities, like American University, Boston University, and many others. The dream was nearing reality, but here I was staring at my 2-year-old son who was groaning in pain and anguish. If you know me, you might quickly presume what I did—I prayed my heart out asking God to heal Wesley T. Mudambanuki.

Remember Mark 10:16, which states, *"And He took them in His arms and began blessing them, laying His hands on them."* As the scriptures teach us, I laid my hands upon my son's head. I had seen the elders within my United Methodist Church doing it repeatedly during worship services and revival meetings. My late mom also did this to her children when they got sick, and it worked for them. The point is that I laid hands on Wessie and believed that God was going to heal him. The night was truly prolonged and tedious; fear overwhelmed me as I failed to understand what had transpired that Friday. I suffered internal anxiety and was physically and emotionally drained. I kept praying, saying, "Lord, please have mercy on my son." I kept the momentum of prayer yet was scared about the imminent sickness. One would wonder whether I still had faith in God at this juncture. Yes, I did; however, fear of the unknown still overwhelmed me.

I woke up the next morning shaking and panicking as I realized I was now in the middle of a huge storm—my beloved son was sick. I carried him to the nearest clinic seeking help. To be honest, nothing tangible or fruitful happened. It appeared that I had now entered the devil's territory as I experienced all the negatives from one of the nurses at this clinic. I walked back to the parsonage uphill, having shortness of breath because the situation was worsening. The waves of sickness were huge and hit my son so terribly.

A thought came to mind of visiting our family friend's doctor who worked at Old Mutare Mission Hospital. I thought, "Yes, this will be the best solution." I drove to Old Mutare Mission, where my son was admitted for several days. I wondered a thousand times how I ended up in such an ordeal. Where is God? Why did He allow this to happen to me while I was preparing to go to America? These were profound questions within the inevitable reality that my son was so sick and depreciating physically. This doctor could not continue helping me, and he referred me to a specialist in Mutare who was well known for his expertise in helping children. My heart cheered up, and I thought something incredible was going to happen.

I want you to know that faith lives amid stormy situations. Storms are unstoppable for us all. What I have realized is that I had to believe in the presence of the omniscient, omnipotent, invisible, and loving God. I had to put on the shield of faith to quench the flaming arrows and darts of the evil one. I say this because, on the painfully long night of November 28th, I had slept on the floor crying to God to heal my son, and my son was not talking back to me each time I called his name. I cried like a baby and prayed like Elijah on Mount Carmel. Indeed, the Bible states that Elijah was a man like us—he suffered during the time of the great famine, praying to God fervently, and in the end, it rained. The Apostle

James seems to encourage us to pray and keep the faith regardless of the intensity of our situations. That sounds so easy, and yet, it is difficult to do when amid such a harsh reality—I had prayed and was still praying.

Early that morning, my late mother showed up and saw how worn out I was. She looked intently in my eyes and said, "I am so sorry you are going through this valley; just hold on to Jesus. Keep the faith and stay connected to God." We held hands as she prayed, and we cried together, looking at my sickly son. That afternoon, the specialist referred us to a private hospital in Mutare, which at the time was the Murambi Hospital, located on the main street in the beautiful city of Manicaland. Oh, my! We had gone in circles for almost a second week without any sign of improvement, and we were tired, but I agreed without any thought other than God was going to intervene and heal Wesley. I was very surprised by the trend of events. The facial looks of the health professionals who were helping me and the whispers from others about my son's sickness indicate something more; even some death predictions were mouthed during the conversations I could hear. I could not believe this because my prayers focused on Wesley's healing.

I did believe I served a God of miracles, signs, and wonders. I was reminded of the Bible story about Jairos and his plight with his 12-year-old daughter who was sick. Jairos came pleading to Jesus, with good intentions, for the healing of his daughter because he had faith in Jesus amid his storms. Jesus agreed to go to Jairos' house to address his situation; however, there was a delay in going because of the woman with the issue of blood. She had also found an opportunity to strategically interrupt Jesus when she touched the hem of Jesus' garment, stating in Matthew 9:21, "If I only touch the hem of his garment, I will be healed."

Indeed, it is understandable to bear with her if you think of her 12-year flow of blood. She had to do what she thought was good for her problem. Truth be told—a miracle happened. In Luke 8, we learn that Jesus asked who has touched Him, as this nameless woman shivered amid the crowd, and she is healed completely by Jesus. It was truly good news for the woman with the issue of blood, though at the same time, we hear that Jairos finds out his daughter has just passed away. That is a sad story to comprehend, especially when one has expectations for healing. The good news is that this story goes on, Jesus prays for the deceased daughter, and she is brought back to life. What a miracle it is for the Jairos' family that their 12-year-old daughter lives again.

I kept on reading these scriptures to revive my soul and faith. I also had read the story of Job the prior month, October, and was painfully devastated to hear of his suffering. I later realized I was in a terrible situation mentally, physically, and emotionally. I tried to find a secret place to hide my feelings and emotions, but there were none to be found. This worsened on December 4th, when I noticed that my son's stomach was swelling, and white stuff filled his mouth. I carried him to a little porch behind his hospital room, and I cried to God, asking for mercy to no avail.

The day went by so quickly, and people were coming from various directions to soothe me in this storm. Nothing made sense to me, and I did not want to be around people who were not in my storm. People tend to try to associate your problem with their own feelings and thoughts, especially when they say, "I know what you are going through," or "It is the will of God for your situation." Perhaps, even as a pastor, I have said that many times to my parishioners through ignorance and without understanding. To be honest with you, dear ones, I ask that you never say such words because you do not know what someone is going through. It is an internal struggle and situation. It is an inner struggle between the soul and God.

One might ask when we can place the will of God in a situation, and I truly believe that this is a deep thought or insight to talk about in human circles. Did God allow Wesley to suffer in such a devastating condition? I remind you again that it was difficult to place a finger on whether it was the will of God, or the enemy had played a part in the whole thing. What happened? I kept grappling with that in the inner chambers of my heart. I knew the devil was a liar, I prayed, and yet, reality stood before my naked eyes, which seemingly were covered by a prescribed lens. My son, Wesley Timu, was dying—I saw it happening before me and denied the reality.

That Friday December 4th, I gathered momentum to pray intensely for my son—I had courage and feared no one. I was so vulnerable as a pastor of a big congregation; people knew about our breakthrough of coming to America. I went to the bathroom and knelt in anguish and tears. This reminded me about Jesus' prayer in the Garden of Gethsemane. It was a tough prayer for Him as He felt the torment of death and pain. There I was, in a little bathroom, deeply immersed in prayer again. I hardened my knees on the flood, sought tissues to wipe my mucus mixed with tears. It was around 2 a.m., and I heard a groaning from my son's bed. I stood up and rushed to check on him. Unfortunately, he could not make it. I saw a light shining upon his body as I tried to rescue him. He stretched his hands and feet and breathed his last breath. It was so vivid as I touched his cold body. The 2-year, 9-month, 20-day-old boy had flown away to be with the Lord in heaven. Quickly, I remembered the words of David after the death of his son when he said,

I recited these David words in tears, knowing that death had befallen my life. I was now childless. They called me by my son's name, "Mai Wesley," but this was no more. Emptiness overwhelmed me immediately. Death had robbed me. The rest is now history and memories of my late son. I remember him saying, "Zvakaoma Sekuru Koma," which means, "It is tough, Uncle Koma." Uncle Tongai is the fifth of my six brothers. We lived with him, and he played with his nephew well. During my son's funeral, I said these words to all the mourners: "I have been robbed by the death of my son, but I will keep the faith." My late father said these words I still recall and cherish: "God will give you from the back of your hands." I could not understand his statement because I was so used to receiving from the top of my hands. After the burial was complete, we came to the United States at the end of 1998.

My dream was fulfilled during this terrible unfathomable crisis. I was childless yet the desire to come to America was before me. I left my country, Zimbabwe, in tears, asking God why? When I got to America, reality, grief, pain, and weariness completely overwhelmed me—the five stages of grief pounded within me daily. One day, I went out in the forest to seek a secret place to pray to my God. I did, and it was an intense prayer. I left the place and went back to our seminary apartment in tears.

I cannot remember exactly the day this happened, but God visited me in my dreams and vision in July of 1999. He called me by name, and I responded. The room was brightened by a huge light which was not of this world. God promised to bless me with a son. He gave me the name and told me to be ready for this blessing. God is always faithful. I got pregnant that year and gave birth to a bouncing baby in 2000, the beginning of a new decade. God's promise came to fruition as I held on to His Word and kept the faith. He who had promised was faithful and did it accordingly.

As I write to you, I am a testimony of God's doing. I have lived, served, and worked in the United States for more than two decades testifying about the goodness of the Lord. Setbacks are inevitable, but God is faithful. Storms of life rage and mount in our lives, but faith in God anchors us tight and strong. My dream to come to America has been marred with tears, sadness, and imaginations of my son, who was supposed to be 28 years old in 2024. God is still carrying me through each storm, and I hold on to His right hand as I sing, "On Christ, the solid rock I stand; all other ground is sinking sand." This is my story of *unwavering faith during storms*.

Reverend Ever Vennah Mudambanuki

Reverend Ever V. Mudambanuki discovered her call to ministry during her adolescence. She could not grasp the call to ministry and ingrained psychological views that were deeply embedded in her life sleeves. Indeed, God had set her apart to fulfill the Great Commission. The call to ministry began in her native country of Zimbabwe and later extended to her dream land of the United States of America. This was an amazing journey which involved deepening and broadening her education in a foreign land. Courageously, she has earned two master's degrees in divinity and psychology.

As a result of expanding her education, she has served in various states and communities preaching and teaching the living Word of God. The integration of ministry and psychology has played a pivotal role in reaching diverse populations, including her native Zimbabweans. She was inspired to begin a prayer line in 2009, which helps her indigenous people to worship in their native language. Souls have been renewed, refreshed, and restored through this wonderful work.

Preaching, teaching, and speaking engagements are performed passionately in her life. The lessons she learned from her late mother propelled her to widen the horizon of greatness in her life. She understands the importance of destiny and strives to always live with purpose. She is a unique vassal of God who dares to live gracefully with humanity as a gift to others.

Her spare time is spent gardening, writing, dancing, and mentoring. Cleaning and cooking have always enlightened her home skills, and she loves to host guests and family. She finds traveling to beautiful historic places fun and does it whenever opportunities and resources are available. She loves to contend in prayer and fasting. Life is never easy, and prayer remains the channel to invoke God's presence in her life daily.

Email: *evavmudambanuki@gmail.com*

Chapter 16

Conquering Fear: The Rhythm of Faith Through Life's Seasons

By Jessie Muzvidzwa

To one who has faith, no explanation is necessary.
To one without faith, no explanation is possible.

– Thomas Aquinas

Fear and faith are both powerful emotions that influence our thoughts, actions, and beliefs, but they operate in different ways. Fear often arises from a sense of vulnerability or uncertainty about the future and leaves one feeling anxious and tense. We try to escape fear by avoiding the source of it. On the other hand, faith is characterized by trust and confidence in something or someone beyond oneself. It involves believing in the unseen or unknown, often based on one's spiritual beliefs. Faith directs attention towards positive possibilities and outcomes. In essence, fear is a response to perceived threats and tends to restrict or limit us, while faith is a response to trust and belief, and therefore, empowers and inspires us to move forward despite challenges or obstacles one encounters.

As I navigate through my own life experiences of when fear gripped me, I am hoping that I can demonstrate to you, the reader, that fear happens to all of us. As I share my personal anecdotes, relevant quotes, practical exercises, and reflection questions, my intention is to illustrate practical strategies and insights that you can apply to your own life. The exercises and reflection questions at the end of this chapter are designed to encourage introspection that can lead to growth, lead one to take action, help one embark on their own journey, and aid in conquering any fear that might arise through the victory of faith.

Embracing the Seasons of Life

Living your dreams means one is actively pushing forward and pursuing their goals, aspirations, and desires. It involves taking steps to make the vision for your life a reality. Each season shapes your journey by providing unique lessons and opportunities for personal growth. When we are fearful, understanding the season we are in can offer perspective and guidance on how to navigate challenges and embrace the inevitable changes that life brings.

As I reflect on my life and am led to share my personal insights, I am reminded of an occasion when fear manifested itself in an ugly way. My experience can best be viewed as having distinct seasons, each characterized by different challenges and opportunities, as such experience evoked unforgettable personal fear. Some years ago, I made a life-changing decision, hoping to chase my dream and take the steps to bring the dream to reality. The decision meant me relocating from my home country, a place I had known all my life, to a neighboring country, a place I thought had better opportunities for me professionally. Initially, when planning the move, I was extremely excited at the thought of a fresh start and new beginnings. But the day I made that move, my world seemed to have been turned upside down. The thought of what I had done was daunting, as I realized how mentally unprepared I was for the move.

Suddenly, fear gripped me and left me emotional and overwhelmed. I asked myself what I had done, as my thoughts reflected on the following:

- ***Uncertainty*** —I had so many concerns and questions. Would I be able to find employment or professional opportunities in a new country?

- ***Cultural adjustments*** —Would I fit into the new culture, language, and even social norms? I had not considered this before my move.

- ***Loss of social support*** —My move meant leaving behind family, friends, and my established social networks; the thought of losing these connections left me fearful.

- ***Disruption of my routine*** —Moving disrupts familiar routines and requires adaptation to new environments. This was causing not only fear but stress each time I thought or felt as if everything was new and unknown to me.

- ***Financial concerns*** —The thought of possibly facing financial instability and adjusting to a different cost of living kept me awake at night, and this raised my anxiety and fear of financial insecurity.

- ***Fear of failure*** —As things did not seem to go the way I had foreseen them going or the way I had planned, I began to fear that my relocating may not be what I expected, and I may not be able to adapt to the new environment successfully.

- ***Attachment to my home*** —I realized that I had developed a strong emotional attachment to my previous home, neighborhood, and community, and the idea of not having these familiar and cherished places evoked strong feelings of loss and sadness, causing so much anxiety and fear in my life.

Each of these fears presented different challenges and opportunities that unfolded different seasons in my life. I quickly learnt that in moments of fear, when seasons in your life change, you need to embrace the change and accept what the season offers. It may be a season that calls or offers one to tap into the wisdom gained from past experiences and opportunities to adapt and evolve. Furthermore, I discovered that in my situation, I could resonate with autumn as a season symbolized by a time of transition, reflection, and change. It was a time for me to let go of what no longer served me whilst preparing for an unknown future.

Purposefully, I watched myself transition from autumn to winter, winter to spring, and spring to summer. When confronted with fear, your winter season can teach you patience, resilience, and the importance of inner strength to weather life's storms, articulated best by the Japanese proverb: "Fear is only as deep as the mind allows." As I allowed my mind to be transformed by the experiences, I was able to gain valuable insights into the lessons each life season taught me, such as to move forward and accept change, to embrace the inevitable, and to find meaning in such transitions.

Cultivating Faith

A key to lessons learnt along the journey of turning my dreams into reality was that, in times of uncertainty, I must develop the necessary strategies to manage and overcome fear. As soon as I realized that fear was affecting my thoughts, my emotions, and my ability to cope with the anticipated changes, I had to cultivate my faith. Understanding and addressing these fears became my utmost priority as I realized that relocation comes with many changes, and one needs to draw courage from their faith, build resilience to overcome obstacles, and furthermore, build the ability to adapt to changes that come with the relocation. Faith can provide a sense of meaning, purpose, and hope, influencing coping mechanisms and resilience in the face of challenges. Through life transitions, experience has taught me that faith is a journey that entails continual growth and not a destination.

Actionable Steps

To overcome fear of any form, there are actionable steps one needs to take. The steps shared below, although used in the context of my situation and related to the fear that gripped me because of relocating, can be applicable to any situation where one needs to overcome their fear. These steps to overcoming fear are critical, as they provide a structured approach to gradually confronting and managing one's fears. Each step builds resilience and confidence, ultimately leading to a greater sense of control and empowerment over your thoughts and emotions.

Step 1: Embrace Faith During Life Transitions

Amateurs built the ark, and professionals built the Titanic.

Never be afraid to try something new when you are full of faith. Most important is your passion and dedication when turning your dream into a reality. Have faith that the timing of whatever situation you are facing is divinely orchestrated and that you are being led to where you are meant to be (in my case, relocation) even if it may not make sense at the time. Accept that uncertainties and challenges are part of the journey, trusting that you are being guided and supported by a power beyond yourself every step of the way.

Express gratitude for the opportunity. In my situation, it involved finding gratitude for experiencing new cultures, perspectives, and opportunities and recognizing that this is a blessing and a chance for personal growth. Through prayer and meditation, find inner peace, clarity, and strength amidst the fears and anxieties associated with your situation through the Word of God (Scriptures).

Step 2: Take Courageous Steps Towards Faith

> *Faith is the art of holding on to things your reason has once accepted in spite of your changing moods.*
>
> *– C.S Lewis*

When stepping out of your comfort zone, be encouraged by taking bold steps towards faith despite fear. When overcoming any form of common doubt, address the fears head-on that may hinder your journey towards faith. Finally, celebrate victories as you reflect on moments of triumph over fear and the growth they signify.

Step 3: Embody Faith in Your Daily Life

Faith is taking the step even when you don't see the whole staircase.

– Martin Luther King Jr.

Find ways to integrate faith practices by exploring practical ways to infuse faith into everyday routines. Live with intention by aligning your actions with faith values. Share your faith through challenges and maintain faith during difficult times. Finally, connect with your community and support networks. These will help you sustain your faith wherever you are planted.

Step 4: Lean on Your Faith

Courage is not the absence of fear but the triumph over it.

– Nelson Mandela

Build inner courage to confront fears and take bold steps towards your dreams. Build resilience to overcome obstacles, bouncing back from setbacks and persevering through adversity. Build unwavering belief in yourself to pursue your dreams and develop the ability to overcome challenges through faith and determination. Be empowered—take control of your fear, transform your mind, and create positive change through action and self-belief. Finally, instill a sense of hope in yourself that you have the power to shape your destiny through faith and perseverance!

Step 5: Celebrate the Fruits of Faith

Do today what they won't, so tomorrow you can accomplish what they can't.

– Dwayne Johnson

a) With gratitude, reflect on the blessings and joys that come from living a life of faith. Celebrate personal growth and transformation achieved through conquering fear with faith. Welcome this journey by encouraging further exploration of your faith as you embrace the rhythm of faith through life's seasons. Finally, find harmony and trust in something greater than oneself as you navigate the ups and downs of life and find a rhythm that carries you forward, guiding you through the peaks and valleys of your journey and finding peace and meaning in the journey.

All of the above are valuable lessons that move you towards transformative growth, just as I have discovered in my own fear journey that relocation can provide you with an opportunity for self-discovery and identity exploration as one navigates the intersection of one's own cultural background and the culture of a new environment. Whilst holding onto gratitude for the privileges and opportunities that I had taken for granted in my own home country, overcoming the difficulties and setbacks associated with relocation built my resilience and inner strength to face future challenges with confidence. Above all, relocating brought exposure to different perspectives and ways of life, therefore encouraging open mindedness and a willingness to embrace diversity. I have learned that immersing oneself in a new culture and experiencing life as an outsider also fosters empathy and compassion for others who may be facing similar challenges.

Overcoming challenges such as bureaucratic hurdles, language barriers, and cultural differences enhances problem-solving skills and resourcefulness. It builds independence and self-reliance as one navigates unfamiliar environments and situations. Your dream becoming a reality can feel like summer, a season of abundant fulfilment and vitality, where you reap the rewards of your dreams and efforts and enjoy the fruit of your labor. When fear arises during transitions, let the summer season remind you of your strength and accomplishments, which can provide you with the utmost resilience and confidence to face these challenges.

Imagine your faith as a dance—sometimes you are moving gracefully with the music, feeling confident and secure in your faith, and other times you stumble and falter as you face insurmountable challenges along your way that can present fear, doubt, and the testing of your belief system. In such times, you need to gather a certain rhythm that carries you forward, guiding you through the peaks and valleys of your own journey. When you gather your rhythm of faith, you surrender to the flow of life, trusting in a higher power, finding peace and meaning in the journey, no matter where it may lead you.

Practical Exercises to Help Overcome Fear and Build on Faith

1. **Letter to Fear**

   Write a letter addressed to your fear expressing your emotions, concerns, and intentions of moving past it. In the letter, end with a reflection on how you can reframe your mindset as you take an empowered decision of faith to move past your fear.

2. **Fear Journaling**

   Set aside time each day to journal about your fears. Write down what triggers them, how they make you feel, and any patterns you notice. Challenge yourself to reframe each fear with a statement of faith.

3. **Visualization Exercise**

   Close your eyes and visualize yourself living without fear. Imagine how you would act, think, and feel if fear had no power over you. Use all your senses to make the visualization vivid and compelling.

4. **Gratitude Practice**

   Cultivate a daily gratitude practice by writing down three things you are grateful for each day. Reflect on how focusing on gratitude shifts your perspective and diminishes the grip of fear.

Reflection Questions

1. What are the primary fears that hold you back from living authentically and pursuing your dreams?

2. How has fear influenced your decision-making process in the past, and what steps do you need to take to mitigate how fear impacts this in the future?

3. What role does faith play in your life, and how does it empower you to navigate challenges and uncertainties?

4. In what area of your life do you struggle to trust in something greater than yourself, and what steps can you take to deepen your faith?

5. Reflect on a time when you faced fear head-on and emerged stronger. What lessons did you learn from that experience, and how can you apply these to future challenges?

Jessie Muzvidzwa

Dr. Jessie Muzvidzwa is an Amazon best-selling author of *Broken Crayons Still Color*, banker by profession, and entrepreneur by calling, with over 20 years' experience. She is currently an international development consultant and founder of a fintech company as well as an agro-processing venture. As part of her way of giving back to society, she supports women entrepreneurs as they start on their own business journeys.

LinkedIn: https://www.linkedin.com/in/jessie-muzvidzwa-phd-37483b2a/

Chapter 17

I Am a Miracle

By Zivai Mutsvene-Ndhlovu

*"Fear not, I am with you; be not dismayed;
I am your God. I will strengthen you, and help you,
and uphold you with my right hand of justice."*

– Isaiah 41:10

5 Years Ago: Grand Cayman

Why would my legs disobey instructions from my brain and go sideways instead of forward? And this, two weeks after I left the hospital? At this rate the bounce back would take eternity, I mused. And the miracle that my daughter Jill and her friend Celine always said I was? I didn't see or feel it.

I had just completed a seven-day course of antibiotics for chest pain. Instead of me getting better, new and more serious complications started. I had nausea, vomiting and general body weakness. I thought the symptoms were an effect of the antibiotic and would go away on their own, but that was not to be. My then five-year-old granddaughter, Jade, for children's love of touch, caressed my legs and exclaimed, "Grandma your feet are frozen!

Let me wrap them in my blanket." How would she have known that the blood flow to the legs was compromised?

As soon as Jade fell asleep, I crawled into the closet. I believed I was dying, and decided the closet was a good place to die in. And also, when Jill came back from work, she would not be immediately met by my corpse on the bed. She would call out and search for me before thinking of the closet.

One Night – Three Hospitals

Jill drove me to the hospital that had prescribed the chest antibiotic. I hoped that the hospital could reverse the effects of the drug they had given me. Unfortunately, the staff on duty did not seem to know what to do with me. They said my vital signs were unreadable, but kept me for three hours, then confessed their lack of appropriate equipment for my condition. So why had they kept me that long? I seethed inwardly.

By that time my condition had deteriorated. My breathing was laboured, yet, like Pharaoh's warhorses pursuing the Israelites, my heart galloped all over my chest, back, and neck. Would it break the chest open and fall out, or jump out through the mouth? Would it too drown like the horses, I wondered. The hospital called 911 and in no time, the crew lifted me onto the ambulance, and put me on oxygen. The paramedic accompanying me called out my name all the way to HSA Hospital and I just mumbled in response.

It must have been with a sigh of relief that the ambulance staff wheeled me into the emergency room. A team of medical personnel was waiting for me, and I was immediately catheterized.

Draining of fluids started there and then. Laboratory tests were performed, and x-rays and scan were taken. The emergency physician told my daughter to take a seat, as if to say watch us do our best for your mum, but if she doesn't make it, it's not due to negligence on our part.

I do not know whether I fell asleep, or went into a state of unconsciousness, because when I came to, it was early hours of the morning. An incision on my left neck jolted me awake. I asked why they were cutting me, and they explained it was to administer a life-giving drug. So, I was dying? 12743 kilometres from my home in Zimbabwe? Would my parents and my siblings be waiting for me in the land of the dead? Would I recognize them? I looked at my daughter.

The cardiologist performed a heart ultrasound scan, and the final diagnosis showed:

- My heart was functioning at 15%,
- I had congestive heart failure
- Blood pressure was very low, 76/44 on arrival at the hospital
- Fluid build up in the lungs
- Threat of multi-organ failure

How could I live with these conditions? I asked myself. With such incapacitation, was life worth living? I reasoned death was better, than live and be a burden to the family.

The emergency physician told me they were transferring me to Health City, an environment that was more conducive to my condition. My body language must have reflected confusion, so he explained that they had told me about the transfer earlier. It was probably during one of my states of unconsciousness, I assumed.

Back on the ambulance I met the paramedic who had taken me to HSA. He was glad that I remembered him calling out my name. I asked if he thought I would die on the way to HSA, but he said I was fine, (professional etiquette, I concluded).

The consultant cardiologist and a team of doctors received me at Health City, and lab works, scans and x-rays were taken. The test results confirmed the HSA diagnosis. It was now dawn.

The Intensive Care Unit

I was admitted to the intensive care unit. In all my six decades I had never been in hospital. My body was plugged in from head to toe for monitoring purposes. The numerous drugs were administered through multiple incisions on my neck and hands, because taking them intravenously would be very painful, I was told. I was placed on round- the- clock care. There were seven other patients, all critically ill, and on machines. We lay on our backs, silent as corpses. But none of us died.

 Because I was heavily sedated, I spent most of that first day sleeping. At visiting time Jill woke me up. She had brought pictures of me growing up with my siblings back home. Very thoughtful of her. But would I ever see home? My niece Tina, who shared a love of reading with me, bought me two books. I chuckled as she read the back blurb of each book. Two ICU doctors updated my daughter on my status. I was surprised to see the doctors' station in the centre of the room. How had I missed it in the morning? The doctors were glued to our monitors 24/7, and responded promptly to each bleep. Medical technology!

The support of the Zimbabwean community in Cayman amazed me. They drove 40 kilometres from town daily to visit me. Only two visitors were allowed at a time, so they waited and took turns to come into the ICU. They prayed for me and encouraged me to rest and relax.

On the second day, Jill came in with my sister Tiana, my brother Lynn, my son Gibson, and Pastor Cal. How had Gibson from Canada, Tiana from Texas, and Lynn from Zimbabwe arrived together? They hugged what part of me they could, avoiding tubes and cables. I stared at them with tears welling my eyes up. I was glad they had come, but then my mind raced wildly. Their combined airfares could sustain week long funeral celebrations, spiced with a mix of traditional dances and resurrection hymns. But was that how other dying people thought? I ascribed reasons to the family's coming:

- Lynn, our patriarch, to collect my body and take it home for burial

- Tiana, to pack my belongings for distribution back home

- Gibson, to squeeze my hand like my dear Mother did mine at her departure

- And the Pastor, for the final rites of confession and absolution, in the presence of family!

Lynn noticed the photo album, and pointed out our favorite places: our Homestead Paul Rose, the river Sihande, and our local school, Mpandashango, where I first learnt to write on a slate. I would never see those places again. As if reading my thoughts, Tiana reminded me of the family reunion scheduled for December that year. Didn't she see I was dying? I cried. And as if letting the tears flow freed me, I spoke about my condition. The family acknowledged I had been through a most difficult time. They wished me a full recovery, and expressed their love and care for me. Gibson wiped the tears from my eyes.

There was a slight improvement in my blood pressure and breathing. I was tested for blocked blood vessels but none were found. The family enquired about my condition, and how my legs were still cold, four days since admission.

"The body is a very intelligent machine that knows when there's a crisis," the critical care doctor explained. "As a result, the heart sends blood to the vital organs: the brain, kidneys, liver and lungs. The legs have to wait for when supplies improve," he continued. "Since Zi neither drinks nor smokes, and has no fainting, no dizziness and no blockages, there is a high probability of her recovery. See, we've already started taking down the Christmas tree," he concluded as he pointed to the monitor.

"Thank you for the information doctor, and for your care for Zi," Lynn said.

"You're welcome. Here is my card so you can check her progress." And true to his word, the doctor responded to their calls.

Pastor Cal prayed and the family left. A nurse asked if I was a pastor, and I told her I was not. What indelible sign of his pastor hood had my Father engraved on his firstborn child? In spite of my response, the nurse gave me her name, her children's names, and asked me to pray for them. I was surprised at that request. I had never prayed since I went into hospital because I didn't know what to pray for. Family, friends and the church prayed for me, like the church did for Peter when he was in prison.

On the eighth day I was moved to the ward and it was such a huge relief. I took a shower and not a bed bath. Though my legs were weak from lack of use, I walked up and down the corridor. Jill found me walking and excitedly screamed, "Mama! You're a miracle! Miracle Mama!" We hugged and walked to my bed. When the family arrived, they too chorused, "A Miracle indeed!" Though I didn't feel a miracle, I burst into tears. The ward was open to visitors 24/7, and Jill stayed overnight with me.

After four days of observation, I was discharged, armed with the doctor's commandments:

- Take the medications as prescribed
- Drink no more than 1litre or 33-40 ounces or 4-5 cups of fluid per day, (I normally took 4 cups tea, 1 litre water, 1glass juice, and 1 glass wine per day)
- Choose whole grain starches

- Eat protein foods
- Do not stress
- Limit your salt (sodium) intake
- Have plenty of vegetables and fruits
- Avoid carrying or pushing heavy items
- Exercise, take walks, but no jogging
- Get a good night sleep, 7-8 hours
- Maintain a health weight, (I had already lost 30 kilos, and was down from UK size 16 dress to a size 10)

"At your command doctor," I said inwardly. I thanked him and the health personnel for their care. ALIVE, I left the hospital.

And I Bounce Back

"Welcome home Mama! Our Miracle Mother!" Celine exclaimed as Jill walked me from the car. As if on cue, the well wishers chorused, "Miracle! Miracle!" But wait! Was that my eldest grandchild Kay among the group? I was astounded. She ran to me screaming, "SURPRISE!" We embraced heartily, and Kay led me to my seat. Pastor Cal and his wife Nessa conducted a thanksgiving service, and then lunch was served. The bounce back was ignited.

The first month was demanding as I had to record daily blood pressure averages and readings from the heart monitor, and then take these to the weekly check ups. My body also struggled with exercise and dietary limits. Walking to the gate was like the two-hour climb to the top of Mt Nyanga. As my condition gradually improved, the doctor adjusted the check ups to: fortnightly, once a month, then bi monthly, and once every 3 months. I warmed up to the family reunion back home, and followed the doctor's instructions to the letter.

I flew home that December, and on arrival, at Homestead Paul Rose, I kissed the ground, and breathed in, "HOME AT LAST!" My siblings, their families, and my children and grandchildren swarmed me. We held hands in a circle, as the blood bond reminded each one of us, "You're me and I'm You".

"NOT in a coffin! But ALIVE! On her own two feet! Zi has returned! Look at her! A MIRACLE indeed! God be praised!" my maternal aunt Sarah declared, as she turned me round for people to see. Jubilation and ululation rang out in celebration. The gathering gyrated beautifully in harmony with the drum beat and the gourd rattles. Cameras clicked from all angles. A pleasant aroma from the copious dishes filled the homestead. Tears of gratefulness rolled down my cheeks. The two-day festivities concretized my bounce back.

"Hi Zi. We heard about the severity of your illness, and it's so good to see you've resumed your content writing and online teaching that had stalled. Thanks for sharing your illness experience," Dr Amy said. She too had learnt to write on a slate at Mpandashango. "Your narrative challenged us to the core. Here we're. Apart from our bi-monthly voluntary visits to the local clinic, we haven't done much to improve the services. One elderly woman asked why we couldn't have the service you got," Amy added.

"Thanks for coming, Amy. Yes, I've resumed writing and teaching, and I'm taking online digital literacy courses for adults. My content has improved as a result," I admitted.

"Well, it's good for you to analyse the situation. Hopefully, you can take action. But we appreciate your regular visits," remarked, John the village head, putting down his calabash of the traditional brew.

Doctor Michael responded, "Action is the reason we're here. We have decided to fundraise and to appeal to donors for infrastructure development and medical technology. Our wish is to expand the clinic into a hospital with doctors. This may take years to accomplish as we'll need to rope in people across disciplines and jurisdictions. Still, it's important that we start, and others may take up after us."

"It's good of you to think of your community so constructively. The villagers can mould bricks and offer their labour as, and when needed. We're so proud of you our children," John asserted.

"Hooray! Our very own hospital! Then we won't have to travel the 62 kilos to the district hospital!" aunt Sarah exclaimed. "And Zi, my daughter, how do you feel about this development?"

"Amy and Michael have a grand vision. My imagination is already scaling mountains: the benefits to our lives, and to neighbouring communities. Would the hospital grow to a nurse training centre? Jobs for the locals?" I responded. "I went into hospital without hope of coming out alive. How such wonderful news fuels my Bounce Back as I look forward to the envisioned hospital!"

"The ripple effects of your MIRACLE, Zi," Michael concluded.

Zivai Mutsvene-Ndhlovu

Zivai-Mutsvene Ndhlovu is a Mberengwa-born Zimbabwean national living in George Town, Cayman Islands. She is a teacher by profession and holds a Bachelor of Arts degree from the University of South Africa, majoring in English and sociology with minors in psychology, geography, and public administration. She has loved reading, writing, dance, and drama since early childhood.

For more than three decades, Zivai has taught English and literature up to the advanced level at schools in Bulawayo and Harare in Zimbabwe. Over the years, she has received accolades for academic excellence, debate, public speaking, and her involvement in the environmental awareness club. Most members of the environmental club pursued careers around the environment and climate, and she is grateful to see the global effect that the club has had.

On retirement from classroom instruction, Zivai went into content writing and online tutoring. She possesses advanced creative and academic writing skills that are employed for content writing, including articles, ghostwriting, blogs, reports, and essays. Her client base includes students, individuals, and organizations. She is a meticulous and analytic writer and never misses a client's deadline.

Zivai's deep love and content knowledge of literature and English derived from her voracious reading, combined with her teaching of all genres from the Americas, the Caribbean, Europe, Asia, Australia, and Africa. The teaching experience was truly enriching. During her free time, she plays Roblox, Fortnite, and board games.

Chapter 18

Simply Me

By Tressa Perry

To accomplish great things, we must not only act, but also dream; not only plan, but also believe.

– Anatole France

I am very excited to share the article below that was published on a platform called Vocal—a platform that has allowed me to be me and conquer my fear. This article has opened many more doors than I ever could have expected. This is the story that helped me dive into my passion and fully embrace my true self....

I'll start off by saying that if I had to choose a word for this next year on Vocal, it would be *"discovery."* I have enjoyed writing for as long as I can remember, and Vocal has been the breakthrough for this passion of mine. As a child, and into my teens, I loved writing poems and song lyrics and eventually started writing fictional love stories. Once I became an adult, though, life hit me like a freight train. Writing fell on the back burner for many years even though I still had a desire deep down to continue it.

I had always let life get in the way until, in my early 30s, I ran across the Vocal platform. A spark lit back up inside of me—just a small one because, unfortunately at the time, I was stuck in an unhealthy addiction which consumed my time and energy. Still, I signed up for the yearly subscription and started to write—a lot, for months, in fact. Sadly, though, a year down the road I looked at my progress, and all I had to show for it were a bunch of unfinished drafts.

I was going through so much that I didn't really have the ability or attention span to commit myself to what I so badly wanted to do. With that being said, and before I can talk about my goals and aspirations for this new year on Vocal, I need to give you a bit more insight into my past. I have two amazingly beautiful daughters; they will be 14 and 16 this year. Due to my addiction, I lost them several years ago. I did, however, go to a treatment program for nine months, worked my ass off to become a better person, and won them back. That was one of the most fulfilling moments of my life. Still, I was a single mother, and life started to kick me in the face again. Long story short, I was not in the position to pay for after-school childcare, and with my full-time job, my girls were at home alone for a bit after school. Besides the fact that it was already a sketchy school, some things ended up happening at home while I was still at work, which made me realize I needed help.

At the time, their paternal grandparents were my only solution. They offered me a deal—they would take them to their city, and my girls would go to school and stay there until middle school, or until I was able to afford childcare. I felt like this was the best choice at the time, but it absolutely crushed me. I felt like I lost them all over again, and it didn't take long before the loneliness and heartache got the better of me, and I slipped up. I ended up getting sober again, but it was a little too late. Their grandma had never cared for me because she wanted her son to marry an LDS woman, and instead, she got me. So, she was all too happy to take advantage of the situation and take custody of my girls. Don't get me wrong, there was a decent period of time when I didn't blame her for doing that.

I was not in the right place to be a good parent, and I'll always be grateful to her for stepping up when I couldn't. Where I struggle with this is that I've been doing well for quite a while now, yet I am still not allowed to see or speak to my girls. It's been several years since I've seen them, and those years are not ones I'm proud of. I was stuck, lost as to where to go because I had always identified myself as "mother." So, without my kids, I really felt as though I had no purpose nor any desire to find one. I got stuck in a deep depression and became stagnant at moving my life forward in any direction. I was just going through the motions of getting through each day.

December of 2022 changed that though. I left a five-year relationship that was dragging me down and decided it was time to start trying to live again. I got back on Vocal six months ago. I deleted all my half-ass drafts and decided to finally put my voice into the world. Writing on Vocal helped me realize how much of an outlet writing is for me; it helps me process and vent in ways that I struggle to do vocally. It has helped me speak things aloud I didn't know how to voice in other ways and has become a great coping method for me.

Part of the reason I relapsed in the past was because I had too many feelings stuffed deep inside myself, and this eventually would become overwhelming to the point where I just needed these feelings to go away. Seeing as I was raised with the belief that we don't express our problems or feelings; I did not have the proper healthy coping tools I needed to get through life in a healthy way. I took the direction I knew. Things are different now, and I finally feel confident in my ability to manage my life and its circumstances without having to numb myself. In fact, I've learned to embrace the struggles and pains in life and use them as lessons to grow into a better version of myself every day. So, writing on Vocal has become a big part of my life that I use anytime I need to let something out.

My health for my age is not as good as it could be. I have cystinuria, which has caused me to pass over 200 kidney stones in my life, and because of that, I have had over 20 surgeries for them. I was warned years ago by my urologist that I may someday have to be put on the transplant list. Learning this about myself has really put some things into perspective and made me realize just how much I've taken time and life for granted.

So, this year—2024—my goal is to spend as much time diving into myself as I can and figure some shit out by exploring who I am as a person and trying to make a name for myself that people will remember. I want to evoke emotion from people and create written pieces that make them really feel this emotion inside. I want to make them question things and see different perspectives. I want to make a lasting impression, so that eventually, when I am gone, people will still come back to read my work.

How does this year on Vocal play into all of this? Well, I plan to use the platform to start to build myself another identity besides "mother." Until my kids are old enough to decide for themselves if I am worthy enough to be in their life, I need to start focusing on myself and who I want to be as a person, especially who I want them to be introduced to if they do choose to be a part of my life again. "Writer" has always appealed to me and been a dream of mine. I have two books in mind that I plan to start writing this year—a personal one, dedicated to my daughters, and a fiction piece that I've had an idea about for the last couple of years.

So, my plan is to use Vocal to really practice and hone in on my writing skills to find where I thrive and find where there can be improvement. I have not yet won a "challenge" on the platform, but I have not expected to either, as I know I still have a lot to learn. I have, though, made "top story" a handful of times, and those moments I cherish because it shows me I'm on the right track. It has helped me with the motivation to keep going and not give up in pursuing this dream of becoming a successful writer.

I have made it a goal to win or at the minimum place in at least one Vocal challenge this year. I don't know if I will enter every opportunity, but with the ones that feel right, I will give it my all. Even if I don't end up winning, I won't take it to heart or let it discredit my work because there are so many other amazing writers who also enter, and it would be irrational to take it personally. I am still going to make the effort though!

I'm so grateful to the Vocal community and how much support I have received from so many people on this platform. Building positive connections is something I've greatly needed in my life, and Vocal has been a wonderful start. I love reading other people's work; there are so many amazing and inspirational writers. They also motivate me to continue to write and strive to push my creative limits. I don't have any pledges yet, but I would like to change that this year by really giving it my all and giving my readers a reason to want to pledge. I've written a couple pieces called, "Letters to My Daughters," and I plan on continuing those letters, as they will be pieces included in the book I'm writing for them. This is a place I find to be a safe space to express my thoughts to them while also perfecting my writing for the book.

As far as my impact on Vocal, I want to make a big impression. I have had a very challenging life and made some questionable choices; many people I have known from a young age have made comments about how I was set up for failure. I want to be open and write about those experiences because I know I'm not alone. I want to share my experiences so people know that making mistakes is part of the human condition, and yet, if you have failed in the past, changing course and finding a better, happier path in life is still a possibility. It's never too late to fight to be someone better. I'm making a choice to break the mold of generational cycles that have run through my family for a long time and break out of old programming that was forced upon me since I was a young child. I'm choosing that no matter what the outcome of my future is, I will have made the most of whatever time I do have left in my life so that I will be able to take my last breath with a smile and a huge amount of love and pride.

Thank you all once again for your support. It truly means the world to me. I hope you enjoyed this piece; I know I enjoyed writing it! Please remember that you're not alone. And keep an eye out for my future book, which will be an extension of this part of my life journey. I think and know you will enjoy it!

Tressa Perry

Embarking on a transformative voyage of self-love and self-discovery, **Tressa Perry** is courageously navigating through past traumas to pave the way for a radiant future. As she progresses along her journey towards becoming a profound writer, Tressa is driven by a heartfelt aspiration to assist others. Breaking free from self-imposed constraints, she is demonstrating that the potential for personal growth knows no bounds and inspiring others to embrace their own journey towards healing and empowerment.

More of Tressa's stories can be found on:

Vocal Facebook: https://www.facebook.com/VocalCreators

Vocal Media: https://vocal.media/

Chapter 19
Faith Over Fear

By Grace Quarshie

"You have been criticizing yourself for years, and it hasn't worked. Try approving of yourself and see what happens."

– Louise L. Hay

Every day, we wake up and have no idea what will happen to us by the end of the day. If we become afraid of this, and we do not move, we will not get where we want to go to in life. This was what happened to me on August 31, 2016.

I had had my usual quick breakfast, arrived at the office, and just settled down to work. The atmosphere was tense in my workplace, spurred on by an impending mass retrenchment program announced earlier that week. One could sense the uneasiness in the air as employees went about their normal work. Over a thousand staff were waiting—anxiously—to hear their fate in the retrenchment exercise.

Thelma, a colleague in the HR department, came to put in a request for water for a meeting she was organizing. As close allies, we performed many duties together as occasion would permit. In this instance, we went together to the company storeroom to fetch the water she had requested for the meeting. I tried to learn in advance what the meeting was about, but she declined to speak of it. She probably had details, yet pondered her own fate just as much and kept mute so this shocking news did not leak. Minutes after we returned, she reappeared at my desk requesting envelopes. Then again and again, she came to fetch one item after the other until all was set for the meeting.

Nana was a coworker who handled issues relating to protocol and was connected to some of the "big shots" in the company. He appeared to have information he could not dare spill. I caught him staring at me in ways that made me wonder what was going on in his mind. Some mates refrained from eating; anxiety had killed their appetite. When my immediate supervisor, Nicole, brought jollof rice and grilled chicken upon returning from one of the branches to which she had gone to perform some tasks, some of my colleagues who would usually be amongst the first to have their turn were missing at the table. It was also at the time of the washing custom (a welcome ritual) for a new recruit, but these colleagues were too tense to partake in the ritual. I was among very few staff who had the guts to still partake in the custom. I was determined not to be broken by the results of the imminent redundancy exercise, whatever they may be.

Similar dullness swept across other departments too. Occasionally, during the day, my colleagues and I would leave my department to crack jokes and lighten the atmosphere in those other departments. There were complacent colleagues too—those who felt they were too important to be sent home. I particularly recall one lady who never seemed bothered, yet later on, she happened to be one of those on the retrenchment list. It dawned on me then that truly any one of us could fall victim. She worked closely with management, and if they would send someone like her home because of their objective, it indeed meant that all of us were at risk of losing our jobs.

Out of a total of eight staff members who sat at the same desk with me, only three retained their jobs. The entire department had only seven people retained out of approximately 17 staff. The departmental leader would meet with HR and then, after a series of deliberations, call the affected staff member into the meeting. My departmental leader was named Ewuradwoa. When you saw an incoming call from Ewuradwoa's number, it meant you were going home. To date, I still freshly recall the proceedings of the moment.

My colleague who had gone out and returned with lunch had food in her mouth when Ewuradwoa's call came through to her. She screamed, "Ajei, m'awu!" meaning, "Oh my gosh! I'm finished!" She went upstairs and came back moments later holding an envelope, probably containing her redundancy package. One's package amount depended on the length of one's stay in the company and the amount of money owed to your employer. After her, one more person—Sheila—was called by Ewuradwoa, and then I received her call too. Ewuradwoa's call sent a chill down my spine.

"Hello Grace, how are you?" Ewuradwoa said in a soft silvery voice. "I'm fine," I responded promptly, anxious to hear what she had to say. "Please, come to the meeting room," her request followed. "Okay," I replied and then announced to my colleagues, "Well, folks, I've been called!" At that, Nana lowered his head and shook it slowly. I walked straight into the meeting room and met Ewuradwoa and one HR staff.

"Well, Grace, this is very difficult for me to do because, having worked closely with you, I know the kind of person you are...." By this time, tears were beginning to well up in her eyes as she fumbled for words. That nearly moved me to tears too, but I was determined to be strong and resisted the urge. "To me...," she managed to continue speaking in a brittle but clear tone, "... you are more of a sister; we're not a boss and a subordinate." She paused again and dried tears from her eyes. "I wish I was not the one telling you this, but... (sobs, sobs, sobs)... what can I do? Do you remember the meeting we had with you on Monday?" "Yes," I said with a nod, trying to maintain an easy, calm posture. "This is the outcome. You are no longer going to be working with us." She had dropped the bomb. I kept my cool and listened silently as she said quite a few more things. "I know you are a child of God. I want to encourage you to not give up. This should not be the end of your life." She sympathized with me, her eyes still wet with tears. "Please, hand over all company properties in your custody to HR."

Just then, I moved to pull off my staff badge, but swiftly raising her right hand mid-air, Ewuradwoa countered my move and said, "No, please, not here. Just hold on a while. Go back to your office and leave it behind, together with any other company material in your possession." The HR staff took turns to speak. "Grace, we are sorry about this. But as Ewuradwoa has said, we hope that you will fight hard and win in life. We have put together a benefits package for you. We have also compiled a list of firms you may apply to for employment. In case you wish to speak with a counselor, we have arranged one who is on standby to hear you out. We urge you to take advantage of these opportunities for the next phase of your life."

When Sheila came back from the upstairs office, she cleared her desk and packed off, handing over her files and leaving immediately. Most of the retrenched staff left that way, and it was the last I saw of them. We didn't even get to say goodbye. I, on the other hand, continued to work till the end of day, leaving the office after 5 p.m. Nicole lingered on awhile too; we were engaged in some work. I was handling stuff pertaining to one of the branches I wanted to wrap up before finally leaving. Later, I scanned a couple of files in search of my handover note, edited it, and handed it over.

I never understood why I lost my job, as the days following this incident left me hopeless and feeling rejected and disappointed in myself because I was not able to achieve my dreams of rising to the top of the corporate ladder. It was not until one night when I had an encounter that changed my life and made me move with faith over fear. I remember, after a long night of not being able to sleep and crying, I heard these four questions:

The first question I heard was, "*Grace, where are you now?*" To me, this question was so obvious because I knew where I was—broken, disappointed, and rejected—and that made me cry more. Looking back, I now realize that where we are in the moment does not really matter. Rather, it matters how long we stay in the place of bondage holding us back.

The second question I heard was, *"Grace, where do you want to be now?"* This question started to put a grain of a smile on my face because I knew so well where I wanted to be but also knew I was not there. Have you ever found yourself in that seat before?

The third question I heard was, *"Grace, what do you have to do to get to where you want to be?"* This got me thinking all through the night, and I took out a piece of paper and just started writing. I didn't know what I was writing, and I certainly did not know this was going to become my faith over fear blueprint. It was these second and third questions that gave me the faith not to go back to the job market again but to start my entrepreneurial journey.

The fourth question I heard was, *"Grace, who do you need to get to where you want to be?"* Well, at that time I did not know, but I knew I had to reach out for help and find people who were already on the path that I wanted to start.

Can you imagine these four questions have now become part of my coaching framework, and I have helped over 1,000 women move from fear to faith by starting a new business, writing books, unlocking their potential, and doing things they have always been afraid to do? If you are reading this chapter right now, I want you to know that you can always rise above your current negative state or any situation you find yourself in that you are not happy with. Never allow fear to hold you back—this is a very common slogan I use every day.

In conclusion, let me share a few tips with you that you can use as you make your shifts from fear to faith. To have faith over fear, you must:

1. ***Discover Who You Are***

   What I mean by this is knowing who you are, what you want, and what you do not like about your current state that can be changed by you moving in faith. Start doing something positive to change depending on your circumstances.

2. ***Develop a Plan to Get You to Where You Want to Be***

   This plan should be a detailed plan including how you will use your gifts, believing in yourself and your gifts, building your faith and confidence, and being prepared to be in a state of mind to learn about yourself and new things. Commit yourself to learning every day. Invest in coaching, which will help you shift your mindset to your possibilities, and read about areas you might want to go into. Look and find people who can help you mentally and spiritually and teach you the steps to get you where you want to be.

3. ***Deploy Yourself to Service and to Using Your Gifts***

   You were created with so many gifts inside of you and full of purpose. At this stage, your goal is to be a person of impact, inspiration, and empowerment. This is where you know that whatever you have been through in life, God was using to prepare you for your assignment. You should be able to jump without fear at this stage because you know who you are and what you want out of life. You are an impact maker.

4. ***Create a Demand for Who You Are and What You Do***

You were never called to play small in this world. You might be living in a small house, running a small business, or driving a small car, but you were made for great things. I have also told myself this. It is just a matter of time. With the right mindset, you will be in high demand, and people will be running to you for what you have. All this will be because you chose to have faith over fear.

Grace Quarshie

Grace Quarshie is an empowerment conference speaker from Ghana, West Africa, a personal and business development coach, and the author of I *Kissed My Job Goodbye: How I Went from Joblessness to Owning a Successful Business and Living a Fulfilled Life*, a book she self-published in 2020 during the COVID-19 pandemic. She is also the founder of Global Life Empowerment Academy Limited, a training and personal development institute for African women, and the African Women Global Community, a platform that connects African women across the globe for collaboration, personal and business growth, exchange women empowerment events, and business networking programs.

From a laid-off employee to becoming an entrepreneur, Grace's resilience and determination have inspired many women worldwide and empowered them to overcome their own fears and self-sabotage to become the woman they want to be. She is an expert in empowering and equipping African women to unleash their possibilities and full potential by monetizing their expertise, experience, speaking, and writing their stories to create global impact. She has trained over 500 women to experience this through her coaching framework—discover your possibility mindset, develop your unique tool, deploy your gifts, and create demand for your gifts. As a result, her clients and audience experience a total transformation that moves them from where they are to where they want to be in life.

Grace has co-authored two books—*My African, My Identity: Stories of African Heroes* and *Dare to Rise Above Mediocrity*, which features the legendary motivational speaker Les Brown—as well as published an anthology of stories with six African women from different parts of the world. She has been featured on national TV, radio, and global platforms, speaking on issues relating to having a possibility mindset, leading with your story, transformation, overcoming fear and self-sabotage, building confidence to achieve your dreams, and having resilience to bounce back after a setback.

Grace was awarded "Community Engagement Personality of the Year" by the African Women in Finance Magazine in 2021, "Woman in Coaching and Mentoring" by the Woman of Stature Global

Awards in 2022, and "100 Most Successful Women Entrepreneurs in Ghana" and "Top 40 Global Brands in Africa" in 2023. She is on a mission to inspire, empower, and equip 10,000 African women to overcome the self-sabotage and fear that is stopping them from taking steps toward their biggest dream and making a global impact. She is passionate about helping African women experience unlimited success in their lives, careers, and businesses and become global brands. Grace is married to Pastor Chris Quarshie, and they are blessed with a champion son, El-team Christan Quarshie.

Website: www.gracequarshie.com

Instagram: https://instagram.com/gracequarshiee

Bio link for all programs and events:

https://bio.link/gracequarshie

Chapter 20

Faith Over Fear –The Journey to Freedom and Liberation

By Dr. Stem Sithembile Mahlatini

"The greatest act of courage is to be and to own all of who you are — without apology, without excuses, without masks to cover the truth of who you are."

– Debbie Ford

I am going out on a limb writing this chapter as we get to the end of this amazing book. I am also skeptical, as I have carried some fear of writing about faith again. When I wrote my first two books, *It's Time to Shift from Fear to Faith* and *The Power of Prayer*, I had a few people who wrote to me and literally bashed me for imposing my faith on them in my books. How could they do this? They were email subscribers who did not believe in God—that scared me.

I, however, felt the need to write this chapter because of the title of this book: *From Dreams to Reality—Faith Over Fear*. I felt the need to walk the walk and write about faith over fear. If you are not a believer and this chapter offends you, I understand. I would like to share this chapter with those who are seeking more encouragement to help them walk by faith and not by sight. If it was not for my faith, I do not know where I would be today. I am so happy and blessed that I have and continue to walk by faith and not by sight. My hope and prayer is that this chapter will strengthen your faith as you walk through this one life that we all have.

What Is Fear?

We have all heard the phrase, "There is nothing to fear but fear itself." However, I think we all know what it is like to legitimately fear something or someone. Fear is our mind's reaction to a perceived threat, and it comes in all shapes and sizes and affects people in different ways.

What Does Faith Over Fear Really Mean?

To me, having faith over fear involves considering the situation, weighing the options, and understanding the danger but then making the choice to fight through the fear and trust God anyway. It means pushing our fear to the side and replacing it with faith. From the time I was in Zimbabwe, growing up in the small township of Kambuzuma, I learned that life is not for the weak. I learned that having the Lord on my side will help me through the ups and downs of life. I learned that my faith in God has to be stronger in order for me to live a stressless and fearless life.

Having faith has encouraged me to trust God and His promises rather than succumb to fear or doubt. Being patient and waiting on Him has been my challenge, and I have written about this challenge in almost every one of my books. I get it now—God wanted me to wait so I could be more mature in Him; He was also preparing and putting together the best plan for my life. Coordinating the *Bounce Back* book series and the Bounce Back Empowerment Conference are definitely both dreams come true and symbols of my faith over fear.

People talk a lot about fear, and many a time I find that fear is a natural feeling that we all have felt at one time or another. Fear doesn't necessarily indicate a lack of faith. Sometimes, it signifies a lack of feeling safe. Choosing faith over fear is a journey we embark on and cultivate as a discipline, which strengthens us in the end.

Having faith in God over fear means trusting in God's plan and provision, even in the face of uncertainty, difficulty, or danger. It involves acknowledging and facing our fears but not allowing them to control or consume us. Instead, we choose to focus on God's promises and His character, believing that He is faithful and loving and that He is with us through every circumstance. Faith in God allows us to find peace, hope, and courage even in the midst of fear and to live with a sense of purpose and meaning that transcends our present circumstances.

Embracing Faith Over Fear

Fear to me has always meant three things: Fear is physical, fear is spiritual, and fear is emotional. Therefore, embracing fear allows me to securely feel physically safe, spiritually safe, and emotionally safe. To fully embrace faith over fear, understanding the various aspects related to fear is necessary. I believe when you understand the different types of fear, it becomes easier to master and embrace faith over fear.

Understanding the Different Fears

In general, fear is a powerful and complex emotion that can manifest in various ways in our lives. Here are some common types of fear and how they may show up in our life:

1. *Fear of Failure*

Fear of failure can show up as procrastination, self-doubt, and lack of confidence.

2. *Fear of Rejection*

Fear of rejection can show up when one avoids social situations or new relationships to prevent the possibility of being rejected by others. It can show up as people-pleasing behavior, constantly seeking approval and validation from others to avoid being rejected. For some, fear of rejection may manifest as difficulty in expressing one's thoughts, feelings, or needs openly and honestly out of fear of being judged or rejected by others.

3. *Fear of the Unknown*

This fear usually shows up as anxiety and worry about the future. To some, it shows up as overly controlling, where individuals may try to exert excessive control over their environment or circumstances in an attempt to reduce uncertainty and minimize the fear of the unknown. I have heard many express this fear showing up as resistance to change or reluctance to step outside of one's comfort zone. I have experienced this fear because I am one of those people who usually prefers the predictability and familiarity of the known over the uncertainty of the unknown.

4. *Fear of Success*

Fear of success is when you have an ongoing fear of succeeding, so much so that you might be inadvertently self-sabotaging. It's not that you think you're incapable of succeeding, but rather, it's more about the fear of change that may come from success and knowing whether you're up for it. For example:

- You might get extra attention, but you're shy or introverted and uncomfortable with the spotlight.
- Public success may bring social or emotional isolation.
- Your achievement might alienate your peers.
- People might think you're bragging or self-promoting yourself.
- You fear being knocked off the pedestal you didn't want to be on in the first place.
- Success may not be all it's cracked up to be.
- Success might change you but not for the better.

Fear of success can be easily confused with fear of failure because either one can keep you from reaching your full potential. Fear of failure has to do with beating yourself up when you think you've bombed out. Fear of success is more about anticipating how other people will react to your triumph. Fear of success can also be referred to as "success anxiety" or "success phobia."

What Does the Fear of Success Look Like?

Fearing the consequences of success can manifest in subtle and obvious ways, such as:

- *Low goals*—You set the bar low to keep yourself from being challenged.
- *Procrastination*—You stall just enough to let opportunities pass.
- *Perfectionism*—You strive for perfection, and when you inevitably fall short, that's reason enough not to proceed.
- *Quitting*—Just when you're on the verge of success, you find a reason to quit.
- *Self-destructiveness*—Substance abuse and other self-destructive behaviors may serve to derail success.

Any of these behaviors can keep you from realizing your full potential and cause fear of success.

Why Do People Have a Fear of Success?

The reasons for developing a fear of success vary from person to person and can be rather complex. Here are a few potential reasons:

Backlash Avoidance

Researchers call it "backlash avoidance" when traditional gender roles lead to a fear of success. In many cultures, men are applauded for their successes while women who achieve the same thing are socially penalized. Women are discouraged from appearing aggressive or to promote oneself in favor of modesty and compliance with gender norms. Some women fear that success will lead to attacks on their femininity or being labeled unlikable and underserving.

Imposter Syndrome

Even people who appear confident may have their doubts. When success comes with increased attention, you may wonder if you can live up to expectations. What if people don't think you deserve it? What if people think you're a fraud? Fear of success can be fear of being knocked off an imaginary pedestal. Imposter syndrome is not a psychiatric diagnosis. It is a syndrome that is experienced equally by men and women.

Childhood Experiences

Childhood experiences stick with us for life even though we're not always aware of them. If, as a child, you were belittled for success or scolded for showing off, it probably knocked the wind out of your sails. You learned to avoid success rather than face negativity. Childhood trauma is a perfect setup for the fear of success to continue into adulthood.

Overcoming the Fear of Success

As I mentioned, one of the things that has helped me is my faith. I will share in this chapter, however, that faith without works will not work. I had to do some work on challenging my limiting beliefs. At first, I did not understand what limiting beliefs were. After I did the work, I realized how important it is to be both a faithful believer and someone who commits to making time to work on challenging limiting beliefs. Let's talk about limiting beliefs.

Understanding Limiting Beliefs

A limiting belief is a thought or state of mind that you think is the absolute truth and stops you from doing certain things. Limiting beliefs don't always have to be about yourself either. They may be about how the world works, ideas, and how you interact with people. The sad thing is cultural values from our upbringing could also be the source of our limiting beliefs. How? In the work I did on myself, I realized that I exhibited more of a fixed mindset because of the values I was raised with and the beliefs that were imposed on me. Limiting beliefs can change your life, but unfortunately, not always for the better. Limiting beliefs can create self-awareness that stops you from chasing after your dreams, forming healthy relationships with people, and creating change in any area of your life.

Breaking Free—Challenging Limiting Beliefs

Challenging and reframing limiting beliefs is a powerful way to break free from self-imposed barriers and reach your full potential. It is so freeing to understand your own limiting beliefs; however, it is ongoing work to recognize and challenge them each time they show up.

The following steps are how I have challenged my own limiting beliefs. My hope is that this will be a guide to help you identify, challenge, and reframe your own limiting beliefs.

1. ***Identify Your Limiting Beliefs***

    - Start by becoming aware of your thoughts and beliefs, especially those that make you feel stuck or hold you back.
    - Pay attention to recurring negative thoughts or self-talk that undermine your confidence or prevent you from taking action.

2. ***Question Your Beliefs***

    - Challenge the validity of your limiting beliefs by asking yourself questions like:
    - Is this belief based on facts or assumptions?
    - What evidence do I have to support this belief?
    - How is this belief helping or hindering me?
    - Would someone else see this situation differently?

3. ***Seek Evidence to Dispute Your Beliefs***

    - Look for evidence that contradicts your limiting beliefs. This can help you see that your beliefs are not absolute truths.
    - Consider past experiences where you have succeeded or overcome obstacles despite believing you couldn't.

4. **Reframe Your Beliefs**

    - Once you have identified and challenged your limiting beliefs, reframe them into more empowering and realistic statements:

    - Replace negative self-talk with positive affirmations.

    - Focus on your strengths and past successes to build confidence.

    - Acknowledge that setbacks and failures are opportunities for growth and learning.

5. **Practice Self-Compassion**

    - Be kind to yourself as you work on changing your beliefs. It's normal to have doubts and setbacks along the way.

    - Treat yourself with the same compassion and understanding that you would offer a friend facing similar challenges.

6. **Visualize Success**

    - Imagine yourself achieving your goals and living a life free from limiting beliefs.

    - Imagine yourself feeling confident, capable, and proud of your achievements.

    - Take time to visualize yourself successfully navigating new experiences.

- Visualizing success can help reinforce positive beliefs, motivate you to take action towards your aspirations, help boost your confidence, and reduce anxiety.

7. **Take Action**
    - Break down your goals into smaller, manageable steps and take action towards them.
    - Celebrate your progress and achievements, no matter how small they may seem.
    - Remember that change takes time and effort so be patient with yourself.

8. **Cultivate a Positive Mindset**
    - Focus on the positives in your life because, at the end of the day, you are all that you have.

9. **Challenge Negative Thoughts**
    - Recognize and challenge any negative thoughts, as they also contribute to limiting beliefs that may hold you back.
    - Replace these thoughts with positive affirmations and reminders of past successes.

10. **Practice Mindfulness**
    - Mindfulness techniques, such as deep breathing and meditation, can help you stay present in the moment and manage feelings of fear or discomfort associated with trying new things.

11. Seek Support

- Surround yourself with supportive friends, family members, or mentors who can encourage and cheer you on as you step outside your comfort zone.

- Having a strong support system can make trying new experiences feel less daunting.

12 Celebrate Progress

- Acknowledge and celebrate your progress, no matter how small.

- Recognize the courage it takes to try new things and be kind to yourself throughout the process.

13. Embrace Discomfort

- Remember that growth often happens outside your comfort zone.

- Embrace the discomfort that comes with trying new things, knowing that it is a sign of personal growth and development.

14: Keep an Open Mind

- Approach new experiences with an open mind and a willingness to learn.

- Embrace the unknown and be curious about what opportunities and lessons each new experience may bring.

- By gradually expanding your comfort zone and trying new experiences, you can cultivate resilience, boost your confidence, and discover new passions and opportunities for personal growth.

I have learned that the power of acceptance and letting go of the need for control is profound and can have a significant impact on how we open up to new experiences and allow ourselves to challenge limiting beliefs as they arise. I have also realized that when we constantly try to control every aspect of our lives, we often experience high levels of stress and anxiety. Acknowledging that there are things beyond our control and learning to let go of the need to micromanage every detail is very important. Knowing this has allowed me to relinquish the need for control, and now I can experience more moments of peace and reduced stress.

When we accept that we cannot control everything that happens to us, we become better equipped to navigate life's challenges and setbacks. Letting go of the need for control allows us to adapt to changing circumstances and bounce back more easily from disappointments. Remember the mindful practice I mentioned earlier? It is very important to find moments to stay present and quiet your mind. Mindfulness meditation is very helpful. By staying present and accepting things as they are, we can respond to situations more thoughtfully and intentionally.

Ultimately, when we learn to accept what we can and cannot control, we gain a sense of freedom like no other. Acceptance brings freedom and liberation. When we let go of the need for control, we free ourselves from the burden of trying to manipulate every outcome and or everyone around us. This sense of freedom allows us to live more authentically, embrace uncertainty, and savor the present moment without constantly worrying about the future.

The power to master faith over fear lies with you. Challenging limiting beliefs and practicing acceptance can help reduce stress, improve relationships, build emotional resilience, increase mindfulness, and increase success. Most importantly, it is free so you get to enjoy a sense of freedom and liberation.

In conclusion, I would like to invite you to publish with us in the Bounce Back book series. I now publish a Bounce Back book yearly and hold a book launch at our Bounce Back Empowerment Conference. If you have ever thought of writing a book, or you are a published author looking to expand your reach, I would like to invite you to be a co-author with us. We welcome you to the Bounce Back author family. Email me at drstem14@gmail.com for more information or connect with me at www.drstemmie.com.

Here is to your success!

Be encouraged!
Dr. Stem Sithembile Mahlatini

Originally from Zimbabwe, Dr. Stem Sithembile Mahlatini is a confidence coach, resident, and owner of Global Counseling and Coaching Services, Inc. and founder of The Empowerment Academy, an online platform with life success programs, workshops, seminars, and books. Her mission is to inspire, empower, and educate others to live stress-free, successful lives through her speaking engagements, books, seminars, workshops, counseling, and coaching services. In addition, she hosts The Dr. Stem Show Radio, Television, and Podcast, which is an educational, empowerment, and encouragement show. You can find her shows on YouTube and all podcast platforms.

Drawing on her background as a licensed psychotherapist, Dr. Stem offers people practical advice on how to tap into their limitless power to change their lives, overcome roadblocks, and aspire to be better than the circumstances that surround them. For businesses, she provides cutting-edge training and coaching programs to help business leaders and employees break through personal and environmental barriers to maximize their success in all areas of their lives. Her lifelong goal is to continue to help others build unshakable confidence to be winners at home, work, and business. Her motto is: "Each day is an opportunity to become more confident, successful, and happy."

Websites: www.drstemmie.com

www.drstemspeaks.com

www.womenyouthservices.com

Ladies—Join me in our exciting, encouraging, and empowering program titled "MyBestLife" on my website www.drstemmie.com. The "MyBestLife" membership for women is a premium lifestyle and wellness program tailored to empower women to live their best lives. By joining "MyBestLife," members gain access to a wide range of benefits designed to enhance their physical, mental, and emotional well-being and their life, career, and business success.

Here are some key benefits of joining the "MyBestLife" membership program:

1. ***Exclusive Community:*** Members become part of a supportive community of like-minded women who share similar goals and aspirations, providing a platform for connection, encouragement, and inspiration.

2. ***Expert Guidance and Support****:* Access to expert advice, webinars, workshops, coaching, and resources from leading professionals in various fields to help members navigate challenges and make informed decisions.

3. ***Discounts and Deals:*** Members enjoy exclusive discounts and access to some of our books, eBooks, audiobooks, and digital products, making it more affordable to invest in their health and well-being.

4. ***Wellness Challenges and Events:*** Regular wellness, career, and business challenges, events, and activities are organized to keep members engaged, motivated, and on track towards their health and fitness goals.

5. ***Mindfulness and Self-Care Practices:*** "MyBestLife" encourages members to prioritize self-care and mindfulness practices through guided meditations, stress management techniques, and other resources aimed at promoting mental well-being.

6. ***Personal Growth and Development:*** The program offers resources and tools to support personal growth and development, helping members build confidence, resilience, and a positive mindset.

Overall, joining the "MyBestLife" membership for women provides a holistic approach to wellness, offering support, guidance, and resources to help women lead healthier, happier, and more fulfilling lives.

Join us and learn more at:

www.drstemmie.com

DID YOU ENJOY THIS BOOK?

If you enjoyed reading this book, you can help by suggesting it to someone else you think might like it, and **please leave a positive review** wherever you purchased it. This does a lot in helping others find the book. We thank you in advance for taking a few moments to do this.

THANK YOU

As a Free Gift to you, I added the following Audio Books Available on my YouTube Channel (DrStem Be Encouraged) for you to listen for FREE.

Subscribe and Enjoy !

- *Beyond The Tears – Bruised But Not Broken*
- *It's Time to Shift- From Fear to Faith*
- *Finding Your True Self*
- *The Power of Prayer*

If you enjoyed reading this book, you might also like the following books available in English and Spanish as Kindle eBook, Audible Audio Book, Paperback, and Hardcover:

- *Unafraid - Stepping Out in Faith: Tips for a Meaningful Confident Life:*
- *Unstoppable – Living a Free and Fearless Life*
- Unstoppable – A Woman's Guide to Self-Confidence
- *Let Your Light Shine: Becoming the Best Version of Yourself*
- *It's Time to Shift from Fear to Faith*
- *The Power of Prayer and Belief*
- *Finding Your True Self*
- *Beyond The Tears: Bruised but Not Broken*

Bounce Back:
From Setbacks to Comebacks

GLOBAL TRAINING COACHING & CONSULTING SERVICES, INC
ORLANDO

www.ingramcontent.com/pod-product-compliance
Lightning Source LLC
Chambersburg PA
CBHW051545010526
44118CB00022B/2580